After reading Phil's book, '.  truly enriched by its content material about the Father fig that I have read such a hear .... we – God's children' embracing hir .... ather. I have been very impressed with the whole connotation of the book to develop within us a deeper understanding of God as our Father. The theme of it being our responsibility to be embracing God, and not just expecting him to embrace us, is well explored by Phil and he explains it in a very sensitive manner that will captivate your attention and truly speak into your heart.

Having known Phil for many years as a Pastor and friend in South Wales, Phil has demonstrated a great love and commitment to the Lord, which has extended very visibly to his family, friends and wider community. Through his ministry in our church he has shown us a great servant's heart as he led us in worship and we were truly inspired to seek the Lord and give God honour and praise.

After Phil moved away we missed him greatly – however he has kept in close contact with us and it has been marvellous to follow him in his walk with the Lord. Not so long ago, Phil went through the 'valley of the shadow of death' after receiving a terminal cancer diagnosis from the oncologists. In the midst of this distressing news he has maintained his Christian faith and love for the Lord.

He has been greatly supported by his wife, family and friends; but following his walk through this valley has been the most inspiring sermon that Phil has ever preached, and the way he has remained true to the Lord has encouraged us to come before God and worship him in a deeper way than before.

This book will encourage the reader to 'fear no evil'. There is grace and power in the Lord to see us through all our walks of life. Our God is able to sustain us to the uttermost. This book is a great enabling tool given by the Lord, for us to more fully understand the Father's heart and His great love towards us.

Dr. Rev Fortunato Santos   **Sardis Baptist Church, Resolven**

EMBRACING THE FATHER

Philip John Amos

Grosvenor House
Publishing Limited

This book is published by
Grosvenor House Publishing Ltd
Link House
140 The Broadway, Tolworth, Surrey, KT6 7HT.
www.grosvenorhousepublishing.co.uk

A CIP record for this book
is available from the British Library

ISBN 978-1-83975-025-0

I dedicate this book to Mike and Carla, without whom it would not exist. Phil.

When he saw the crowds, he had compassion on them,
because they were harassed and helpless,
like sheep without a shepherd.

Matt 9:36

ACKNOWLEDGEMENTS

I would like to thank my family, Carole my wife, for her patience with me when I have suddenly disappeared to ponder and write, and also for meticulously proof reading the manuscript. My daughter Becci, for her gracious help with the use of her computer, not least for their love and helpful suggestions and encouragement in the writing of this book.

Thanks to my friends, Chris and Lynda Osborne for patiently reading the first manuscript, and offering some useful and objective thoughts.

I want to thank Pastor Dr. Fortunato Santos for appraising each chapter of *Embracing The Father,* correcting and critiquing where appropriate, and generally mentoring me in the process of writing this book.

In remembrance, I thank my own Father for his loving care over many years and his amazing theological prowess. My mother, for her gentle spirit and constant support, and my sister for her sacrificial mission to reach out to those most in need in Peru, with the love of Christ.

You have all, in many wonderful ways, demonstrated the unconditional love that our Heavenly Father has for his creation. An inspiration to me indeed!

PREFACE

The motivation for this book came after a Sunday morning, following the teaching of God the Father in a Series on the Trinity. Two friends gave testimony of how it took time and revelation to fully understand the loving Father heart of God.

This might be due to several reasons. It may be that you haven't had a good father figure throughout your childhood. It is difficult to truly see God if a role model in your life hasn't represented his character well. It may be that past sins make it hard to feel that God is really approachable, and that 'the slate has been wiped clean'. Then again, to understand something well requires time, teaching and often testimony. To learn another language for instance will require these three things. After being born again into the new spiritual life that God has given us, they will help us too.

Scripture leads us through a pathway of time, teaching of truth and testimony.

As we mature in our faith, we begin to engage with the Father more, and at a much deeper level. The Bible is never exhausted. There is always something new to learn, however long we have *lived it* or however scholarly we might be, or not be.

He is no respecter of persons, we all walk the same journey, but choosing the best or the right route is of paramount importance.

If you climb one mountain peak you often find another, hidden and higher beyond it. I am a musician, but although I have a passion for music, playing an instrument well doesn't just happen overnight. It requires on going practice. As with much in life, we have to practice. Spiritually we have to 'practice the presence of God'. First we must have the passion, then develop that passion and keep practicing!

CONTENTS

INTRODUCTION

A TOUCH OF THEATRE...

Walking in L'lle Tudy, a peninsular in Finistère, France, in October 2018, I happened across the most stunningly beautiful sunset I have ever seen. The sky was truly copper as was the water, with a line of trees fading to black between the two.

Walking along a bridge with water to both sides and no discernible destination in the distance, I did wonder for a moment whether this was actually the path to heaven. I could only burst out in praise at such a sight, and found no words in either English or French to worship a God who could ever have created such beauty.

I went with my wife Carole, every evening after that to catch that same sky, but although it was beautiful each time it was never quite *that* sunset.

Of course I have the photographs, but can they do justice to actually *being* in the presence of that panoramic view, the lapping of the calm water, the feel of the gentle breeze and their entire impact upon the senses. No, for sure they don't.

It's rather like going to the theatre and watching a film of a Royal Opera House performance. It's the same story, the same singing and the same set, but not the same as viewing it 'live' and really living it and experiencing it in all its glory.

COLOSSIANS 1:15: 'The Son is the image of the invisible God, the firstborn over all creation.'

HEBREWS 1: 3a: 'The son is the radiance of God's glory and the exact representation of his being.'

The ESV tells us: '…and the exact imprint of his nature.'

In a sense my photographs act as an exact imprint or representation of that glorious sunset, just as Jesus is the exact imprint of the Father. However, what is missing in my photos is seeing the whole picture in the perspective of reality and real time. This is what can be missing in our full understanding of the perfect Father heart of God. But Jesus comes to us as the representative of the Father's heart, so that we cannot miss to 'See what great love the Father has lavished upon us, that we should be called the children of God! And that is what we are!' (1 John 3: 1).

It is in the reality of Jesus, who is not like the inanimate image of a photograph, but our living and loving Lord and Saviour, in relationship with God the Father and the Holy Spirit, equal with God himself, who in his own suffering gives us the exact imprint of the character and nature of the heart of the Father.

When we truly realise this, when we see the amazing greatness of God and the pitiful smallness of man, indeed of ourselves, we begin to wonder how on earth we can bridge this great divide. Of course we can't bridge the divide ourselves, only the deep and glorious plan of heaven, made manifest on the earth can achieve such a thing, to raise us up to be like him and to marvel in His presence.

The intention of this book is to draw us into a deeper relationship with our Heavenly Father, to bring us to a greater understanding of who God is, what He is *really* like. Is the God of the Old Testament different to the God of the New Testament? Is that really the same God? Do we read through the Old Testament and when we reach the New Testament exclaim 'phew' and wipe the sweat from our brow and say, 'Thank God for Jesus!' Well actually if we do say that, we have already begun the journey of a fuller understanding that brings Father God closer from our head and into our heart, (or into our spirit). It is not intended to be a book of weighty theology, but simply to lead and guide us into the truth of how the Father *really* cares about you and me.

In 2016 I had a massive seizure, which following MRI scans, was diagnosed as a Glioblastoma. They are diffuse, meaning that they have threadlike elements that spread into the brain. A biopsy is carried out to determine the grade of the tumour, which are from 1 to 4. Although they are all cancerous, the first two are not necessarily as harmful as the last two and tend to be benign. They might not grow into the higher grades or require an operation. Grade 3 and 4 however are malignant and spread very rapidly.

The prognosis of all this is that if you have a higher grade, life expectancy will be shorter, with lower grades possibly not life threatening at all.

It was thought that mine may have been a grade 3, but after the initial operation to remove a small part of the tumour it was discovered to be a grade 4. The highest.

Without further treatment, 6 months would be the expected time to live, and with chemotherapy and radiotherapy, between 12 and 18 months.

A person of 40 years of age would have a median statistic of around 3 years and a person who is 60, perhaps around 2 years following the initial diagnosis.

I turned 60 in the year following the seizure during the period of the treatment.

Treatment symptoms can vary significantly and tiredness or exhaustion would be part of this. Extreme weakness, inability to function normally, headaches, rashes, hair loss, pain and general discomfort along with nausea and mood swings are pretty much the norm, in a list as long as the terms and conditions of an insurance policy!

During appraisal counselling I was offered all of these, but I have to say that in prayer as a family, we decided *and determined by faith* to turn them down as far as was possible.

I will say that some fatigue was evident as was to be expected following such a serious trauma, skin rashes and also hearing issues from the treatment which have all now been resolved. A couple of other symptoms, which weren't on the list, both appeared and disappeared (Blackened fingertips and smelly feet!), which both amused and flummoxed the medics, and have probably now been added to the list....

Now in late 2019, following a recent MRI, there is no visible evidence of the tumour in my brain, whereas 3 years ago, a quarter of my brain was filled with this 'golf ball' size mass. The statistic says that it is incurable. With the treatment that is currently available, it will return. Only 5% of people will live to 5 years with many unable to survive the treatment, of which I know to be so, having witnessed this for myself.

Heaven's statistics are however, different to those of man. Reading healing scriptures, proclaiming the year of the Lord's favour, as bestowed upon us in every moment of every day, and speaking words of faith, in these are the truths and promises that we cling on to, and place our faith and our hope firmly upon.

We are encouraged to do just this in the closing words of the Apostle Paul's letter to the Ephesians.

'Finally, be strong in the Lord and in his mighty power. Put on the full armour of God, so that you can stand against the devil's schemes. For our struggle is not against flesh and blood, but against the rulers, the authorities, against the powers of this dark world and against the spiritual forces of evil in the heavenly realms. Therefore put on the full armour of God, so that when the day of evil comes, you may be able to stand your ground, and after you have done everything, to stand' (Eph 6:10-13).

SECTION 1

THOSE TROUBLESOME TRUTHS!

CONTENTS

Chapter 1.

THE LOVER AND THE LOVED –

Knowing The Father

I have loved you with an everlasting love... Jer 31:3

The prayer of Jesus in John 17 is wonderfully revealing as to both the relationship that Jesus had with the Father, and the relationship that the Father has always longed for with us: His children, His family. It is worth noting here that the gospel of John is the most intimate of the four gospels in the depth and revelation of both Jesus and the Father, and the relationship between them and how we are to be included within that relationship. It was written by the disciple who considered himself to be most loved by Jesus, and had 'a closeness' with him that truly stood out. For example, at the last supper Peter motioned to John, who was reclining next to and against Jesus, what he meant by 'one there who would betray him'. I can imagine him whispering with one hand across his mouth, 'Hey John, ask him what he means? I don't really get it'.

He was also the only one who appeared to have followed Jesus all the way to the cross while others had slipped away. John continues this story of love from the gospel and into his letters, which we will look at as we go on.

Regarding the Fatherhood of God, Jesus speaks of God as 'Father' some 65 times in the Synoptic Gospels and over 100 times in John.[1] So it's from pretty solid ground that we can grow a deeper understanding of the Father's heart into our spirit.

Jesus prays in v.1 – 5: 'Father, the hour has come. Glorify your son, that your Son may glorify you. For you granted him authority over all people that he might give eternal life to all those you have given him. Now this is eternal life: that they know you, the one true God, and Jesus Christ whom you have sent. I have brought you glory on earth by finishing the work that you gave me to do. And now, Father, glorify me in your presence with the glory I had with you before the world began.'

In v. 22-23 – 'I have given them the glory that you gave to me, that they may be one as we are one - I in them and you in me – so that they may brought to complete unity. Then the world will know that you sent me and have loved them even as you have loved me.'

We could almost stop here, read this whole chapter several times and allow the Holy Spirit to open up our mind, our heart and spirit to the Fatherhood of God. However, we shall continue, and hopefully, and prayerfully, engage further with these verses.

Jesus is clear in this passage that he was co existent with the Father and the Spirit before the world was ever created. It is clear from this prayer and the opening chapter of John's gospel, that the Father and the Son together with the Holy Spirit were living in perfect harmony, were glorifying one another and living in a continual state of expressing love to one another: 'I made known to them your name and I will continue to make it known, that the love with which you have loved me may be in them, and I in them' (John 17:26, ESV).

In the 4th Century A.D a theologian named Arius began to teach a theory that as God was the Father, he must have existed as just one God before the Son, that in fact the Son was created, begotten of the Father. (A kind of Jehovah's Witness' stance on the Godhead, albeit with some differences.)

Here is his short statement presenting his view: 'God has not always been Father; there was a moment when he was alone, and was not yet Father; later he became so. The son is not from eternity; he came from nothing.' [2]

His teaching was discussed and denounced at the 1st Council of Nicea in 325 AD.

This would make the Father into a single God, monotheistic, rather like Allah and very distant, for how long we cannot say and with only himself to relate to or indeed to love. To this we have to say, No, no, no. This cannot be!

This is looking at God through the natural human mind regarding Fatherhood, but not through the mind or the eyes of the spirit.

It turns the Godhead into God IS head. A bit like winning the Gold at the Olympic games, you get to stand on the higher podium, whereas the silver and bronze get to stand a little lower. That would then be the position of the Trinity. God is always in the top spot, the C.E.O. - leaving Jesus and the Holy Spirit to do his bidding.

Right at the start of creation in Gen 1, you will see that The Holy Spirit is already 'hovering over the face of the waters' ready to create; just waiting for that spoken

5

word of faith that causes creation to come into being. No, the Father, Son and Spirit are and always have been, and always will be, equally co existent and importantly of shared purpose in *all* that they do and are.

There are plenty of attempted descriptions of the Godhead, the Trinity. I suppose that one of the most well known being that of water. It can be ice, or running water or steam. Well, that must be it. The Holy Spirit is the breath of God, so he must be the steam. Jesus is as water poured out, that takes care of that and leaves the Father as the block of ice; yes, cold and hard. How clever. How terrible! I'm sorry to burst any bubbles over that one if you thought that to be a great analogy. I thought so once too! Again. No, no, no.

Firstly God never changes - Mal 3:6. He is always constant and is the same in all things. Secondly the character of the Father, Son and Spirit is identical; the function may differ. The character remains the same. Jesus declares in John 7:38: 'Whoever believes in me, as Scripture has said, rivers of living water will flow from within them.' This living water is continually flowing from the heart of the Father through the humanity of Jesus, as seen on the cross, where his blood and water was poured out, and by the Holy Spirit in us and through us.

So it's no good to reduce God to our limited ways of understanding. If we want to speak of his character, we can say of God; he is perfect love, ministered in flesh through Jesus and administered in spirit by the Holy Spirit.

Plant Pot Theology...

'Hold on' you may say. 'I thought that we weren't going to get too deeply tangled up in theology!' Well no, that's not my intention but it is important to understand as a starting point, some foundational fundamentals of our faith in order to even begin to understand the fullness of the character and nature of our God.

In gardening if we fail to dig down to the root, we cannot lift the plant and replace it elsewhere and expect it to thrive. If I grow a plant in a pot, I only expect that it will grow as much as the root will allow. I may have to dig it into the ground to allow it flourish further. It is the same in the spiritual sense, to fail to plant the truth deeply and firmly into our heart or let me say into our *spirit*, we also will not grow and flourish, and display the glory that is in the root of the Father's heart for us.

If we only discuss together our views of God based on our limited human knowledge, then those views will be at best, subjective and at worst erroneous. I am not a learned theologian. My PhD is in being a parent, husband and disciple! I simply hope to lead you into searching out the ways of our awesome God and growing stronger for it.

The difficulty that we tend to encounter as we trudge through the tougher texts of the Old Testament is coming upon 'those troublesome truths' that seem to divert us off of the path, or stand in the way of fully grasping this continuing love of God.

How often have you read a piece of scripture and thought that it was all going so well and now this! The fire consumes them or the earthquake buries them all and an entire clan is removed from the earth and it's, 'oh I wish this bit wasn't in here. Now I just don't get God. It seems more about punishment here than rescue, or love, or kindness'.

This is what Richard Dawkins says: 'The God of the Old Testament is arguably the most unpleasant character in all fiction: jealous and proud of it; a petty, unjust, unforgiving control freak; a vindictive, bloodthirsty ethnic cleanser; a misogynistic, homophobic, racist, infanticidal, genocidal, filicidal, pestilential, megalomaniacal, sadomasochistic, capriciously malevolent bully.' [3]

As a believer and lover of God this is a very unpleasant statement to read, but sometimes can we admit that occasionally we have moved toward that direction in some of those adjectives if only marginally, in things that are difficult to grasp, both in Scripture and in the complex and difficult situations we face in life?

This is the problem of neither contextualising scripture, viewing an incident in isolation which only gives us a snapshot of what needs to be viewed in a panoramic form (rather like my seeing the sunset in Finistère in its entirety), and also not viewing it with hearts that have been renewed or regenerated by the gift of the Holy Spirit. That gift however has been given to us and made alive within us.

We will look at a scenario from the Old Testament later that may be helpful for us.

Our spiritual eyes must be opened to engage with God in all his glory. 'Having the eyes of your heart enlightened, that you may know what is the hope to which he has called you, what are the riches of his glorious inheritance in the saints' (Eph 1:18, ESV).

'Open my eyes that I may see wonderful things in your law' David said in Psalm 119:18. (In this book I am taking the view that David wrote Psalm 119. I believe that most people of Jewish heritage would attribute this Psalm to David.)

Better to contrast the viewpoint of a man who neither knows or wishes to know God, with that of Moses who lived and breathed God daily, who lived with the trials of a rebellious people and met with God 'as one who speaks to a friend' Ex 33:11, and when Moses said, 'Now show me your glory,' God replied: 'I will cause all my goodness to pass in front of you.' v.19. It is not possible to separate the greatness of God from his goodness. Essentially they are intrinsically the same. 'The Lord, the Lord, a God merciful and gracious, slow to anger, and abounding in steadfast love and faithfulness' (Ex 34:6b). The New International Readers version puts it: 'I am the Lord, the Lord. I am a God who is tender and kind. I am gracious. I am slow to get angry. I am faithful and full of love.'

God is kind. He abounds and overflows with goodness and truth and longs for that outflow to be both flowing into and out of our lives.

'Hesed'

Hesed is a significant Hebrew word that would mean so much to the Middle Eastern understanding but probably very little to our Western minds. It is so very difficult to fully capture its truest meaning. It refers to a strong loyal love that can never change, it is unrelenting and immutable, as is God's grace toward us, through Christ, but it contains The Father's character and his purpose, it is continually expressed divine favour and scattered across the pages of the Old Testament over 200 times.

It is covenantal unbreakable love that drives Jesus to embrace the cross for you and me, and The Father in turn to embrace his children with such precious care and kindness.

'Agape'

Perhaps we can say that this Greek word, found over 200 times in the New Testament, carries a similar sense as the word Hesed. It is also a sacrificial and continual love that gives all and expects nothing in return. Yet with Jesus, fully God and fully man in the equation, we consider afresh what Agape love truly means for us in our salvation. It just can't help but bring our response. In this, 'Agape' goes even further than 'Hesed' as it involves our hearts poured out in praise and worship to a God who has done it all.

Jesus says to Peter; 'do you really love me' and Peter responds; 'yes of course I do'.

Knowing the Father, or getting to know him in a deeper and more intimate way, is I would suggest, a constant process of faith and learning.

Abraham has an interesting and revealing conversation with God in Gen 18. He asks God whether he would spare the wicked city of Sodom and Gomorrah for the sake of the righteous. (In this case, Lot and his family.) Instead of coming straight to the heart of the matter, he begins with a kind of bargaining approach as if he really isn't sure how far God would go with his blessing. He starts at 'would you save 50' and God agrees, then he moves to 45, then 40, 30, 20 and finishes at 10. Of course God knows exactly where he is going but just waits to see how far Abraham would extend and grow his faith in his understanding of the Father's heart. A Father of whom he is only just beginning to get to know and to trust: He knew nothing about God until he heard the call upon his life, and he followed the call, even though it led to many trials ahead. Of course God would have agreed to saving just *one*, had Abraham reduced the number further. He wouldn't have said: 'Sorry my son, but now you're just going too far!'

Do you recall the parable of Jesus - 'If the shepherd loses one sheep, he will leave the 99 in the country and go after the one until he can find him and carry him back?' I wondered what would happen if another went missing while the shepherd was searching for the first one? Well, you know, he would just go after that one too. Perhaps that doesn't make the greatest sense in our world of 'time and motion efficiency' but God doesn't think in our way. He has all the time he needs for you and me. I have to admit here, like the apostle John, that I am God's favourite! Before you exclaim, 'what an arrogant person you are' - I must add - 'you know what? You're God's favourite too!'.

Chapter 2.

CREATION AND CURSE –
A Perfect God

Be perfect, therefore, as your heavenly Father is perfect.
Matt 5:48

This verse comes at the end of Matthew 5, where Jesus is teaching what would be clearly a new revelation and attitude to the law, and what the cultural mind set and interpretation of the day would have been. The chapter begins with the 'how we are blessed' beatitudes, then teaching of how Jesus was to become the fulfilment of the law himself, and introducing a completely fresh approach to how a person should look at, deal with or treat another. A new level of love, a different understanding of the depth of love that is ground breaking and controversial is introduced and builds toward that final summary which in essence says, 'we gotta be just like God'. Perfect.

I imagine that there may have been some 'wide eyed, open mouthed' listeners that day!

Jesus is really saying that 'If you love others who love you, well anyone can do that'.

That is love with partiality. He is saying that we are to love as God loves, without partiality.

another way to interpret the description 'perfect' in od's world - is simply the word _love_. Agape love.

When asked 'which is the greatest commandment?' 'Jesus replied, "love the Lord your God, with all your heart and with all your soul and with all your mind."' A reference to Deut 6:5, _and oh_, '"Love your neighbour as yourself." All the law and the prophets hang on these two commandments' (Matt 22:37 and 40). (Italics added.)

How do we deal with this teaching, this knowledge that God is a perfect Father and only wants to bless us, and yet requires us to also be perfect _and_ a blessing?

Coming from the position that we are natural, human beings and that God is a supernatural divine being tends to mess with our mind, will and emotions that define us rational thinking people. Have you seen some of those precarious rope bridges that swing backwards and forwards when crossed? For this we need faith. How about being pushed in the wheelbarrow by Charles Blondin along a tightrope? Now that definitely required an act of faith!

However, drawing closer to the heart of Father, or having the Father draw close to us also requires faith. It is only faith that activates the spirit man within us. The spiritual dimension is activated by faith. Faith is the energy, the engine room of heaven, of living in the spirit. Of having minds renewed, our will transformed to be lovers of God, and our emotions connecting with his love through the conduit of the power of the Holy Spirit living within us.

The Power Is On...

I have experienced electric shocks three times now. Yes I was careless. Once in France to test whether the electric fence so commonly used was really 'live'. It was. A bit more power runs through our mains electricity. I grabbed hold of a bare wire under a fridge while doing some DIY work. That one smarted a bit. More recently I received a shock from my kettle base due to the leaky kettle!

I couldn't see the electricity but when it's turned on there is power there. The power of the Holy Spirit is always on. We engage with God as we turn faith on.

'Without faith it is impossible to please him, for anyone who would draw near to God must believe that he exists and that he rewards those who seek him' (Heb 11:6, ESV).

Without faith it is impossible to please God, but God has given us his spirit through Jesus, as we saw earlier in John chapter 17, so that we can believe that God is perfectly good in all his ways and his overwhelming desire is to love, bless and prosper his creation. We will look again at this in the context of covenants in the next chapter.

God created the heavens and the earth through love, by faith. With the spoken commandment by faith, he brought creation into being together with the Spirit and the Son.

What was the last act of creation in Genesis 1? Let's have a think about this. On the sixth day God makes man in his image to have 'dominion' or to take charge of all that he has made up to that point. 'So God created man in his own image, in the image of God he created him; male and female he created them' (Gen 1:27, ESV).

That sounds pretty final but it's not the last thing that God does. He goes on to bless them and this is so important. In his blessing is essentially the first commandment that mankind should be fruitful and increase. Also that he would be the guardian of all that God had created, and God gave everything to man. When God saw all that he had made he declared that 'it was very good' v.31.

Man was to be blessed by God in creation - and God would also be blessed by man through that same creation. That's quite mind blowing to know that we have been created through the love of God, not as servants, not as his playthings, his chess pieces to move around at will in some cosmic game; but as his family, to love and be loved, the offspring of the Father, accepted by the Father and *enjoying* the Father.

Through the landscape of the Old Testament can be seen the all-encompassing purpose of God the Father to this end.

As my foundational statement, I come from the premise that God is perfect in his character and that perfection without flaw can only produce a nature of absolute holiness and infinite love. As the Father of all creation together with the Son and the Spirit, he not only creates, *but also* sustains and blesses all that he has created. We can say equally that love created the world and all that is in it, just as we can say that God created the heavens and the earth. God is love and love is God, in the truest sense. That is to understand that the perfect love of a perfect God cannot be understated. Our human attitude towards the word *'love'* is often fickle, dumbed down, misused and bandied about as liberally as a salt shaker on a bag of chips. We have little understanding of just how deep is the love of the Father who sets in motion a plan of redemption, even at the conception of creation.

We know well that after Adam fell in disobedience that the blessing was unable to continue in the face of a perfect God, and became instead a curse. But God's plan was to begin to restore this blessing through Abraham, and the incredible and ultimate plan of redemptive creation was born.

Gen 15 sets out the new covenant that God makes with mankind through Abraham. Abraham is learning about this God that he is worshipping, and although he cannot comprehend how God can bless an ageing couple with no offspring with any kind of hope or future, he makes a decision to believe God's promises by faith, and God credits righteousness to his account as a result.

Have you ever the felt the hopelessness of a situation that has no recognisable answer to it? This promise to Abraham of trust in the living, loving God is by extension offered to you and to me. 'If you belong to Christ, then you are Abraham's seed, and heirs according to the promise' (Gal 3:29).

A covenant goes further than a contract. Think of a modern day contract like one made for instance with a football manager. If he doesn't perform as expected, the contract is terminated or 'broken'. A covenant in Bible times was made through two parties who pledged with a binding oath to defend one another with their own life, even to death, involving the sacrifice of animals, and walking between the two halves in a 'figure of eight' format, symbolic of an eternal nature and sealed by the mixing of their blood. This covenant, unlike the contract above, has nothing to do with performance, which is fantastic for us, as our performance can never come close to the perfection of God.

Now this is very significant. God didn't walk with Abraham to make this covenant but verse 17 of chapter 15 says that 'a smoking fire pot and a flaming torch passed between the pieces.'

It seems to get a little weird here like a scene in 'Harry Potter' but is actually rather wonderful. The symbolism or imagery here is that of judgement, of holiness, of the relationship of God toward man, and here God is making this covenant together with Jesus through the power of the Spirit on behalf of Abraham and his seed, then to all mankind. Abraham is a bystander in all this. In his humanity he cannot establish this covenant. His mixing of blood won't suffice, only the shedding of the blood of the saviour foreshadowed in this moment will do. God is Divine. He cannot break his promises to us. His word is a binding oath. It doesn't depend on a fallible human being. This covenant is designed to be eternal, infinite, everlasting and without compromise. Wow, *or Selah*: just ponder that for a moment....

God would reinstate this covenant further in Chapter 17. In the promise that Abraham would be a Father of many nations, he introduces his own name into that of Abraham and Sarah. They were up to now actually Abram and Sarai, but here the Lord includes a part of his own name YHWH. They are to carry the very essence of the nature of God with them everywhere they went. Through Jesus, in covenant, we too carry his name and the presence of his Spirit everywhere we go.

God's one focussed purpose throughout the Old Testament or Covenant was to introduce and to bring in the New Covenant, to re establish that unity of Father with son and daughter, you and me, through the mediator, his Son Jesus. The blessing that came through Abraham is for all time and all people, that's *today* friends!

The *Winslow Boy* is a story from the Edwardian era. It's the story about a young lad of around 13 years of age from an influential family who arrives home early, discharged from his school of education having been accused of the theft of a postal order for just a few pounds. The family at first, attempt to prevent his father from knowing this, in fear of the supposed austere nature of father, but it slips out and he demands to see his son, alone. He has arrived home soaked from the rain. '"Why are you wet boy?" asks his father. "I was in the garden father," replied the boy. "Why?" he is asked again. "I was hiding." "From whom, from me?" "Yes" answers the boy. "But haven't I told you, if you are ever in trouble come to me first" says his father.' [4]

Now that's a pretty good picture of Adam and Eve hiding in the garden after they had sinned, conscious of a broken relationship with their Father and unsure of the consequences, now uncertain of his on-going love for them, and aware of the big mistake that they had made.

Actually, whereas the Winslow boy was entirely innocent of the charge against him, in the case of Adam and Eve they were entirely guilty in their disobedience.

In our story, the well respected father who believes in his son's innocence embarks on an unprecedented journey of risk and sacrifice, of family, reputation and career in order to clear his son's name. He becomes the son's mediator, and dedicates his life to this one purpose until the reputation of the family is exonerated.

Have you thought about what the effect of the separation of mankind and God would have meant to him? Gen 3 shows us that God would walk in the garden in the 'cool of the day'. To be close to and in daily fellowship with man was the absolute desire of God. As we love to be with our children, so God loves to be with his.

This is exactly what God has achieved for us through Jesus. Though we were guilty and dead in our sins, running from God and undeserving of his blessing, he risks it all for the sake of our reputation, restoration of relationship together and renewal of our spirit man. It's worthy to note that on the seventh day of creation God rested from all his work. After Jesus ascended into heaven after rising from the dead, he ascended to the Father and sat down at his right side. God restoring his creation, Jesus paying the ultimate price for our sin, and the Holy Spirit 'hovering' again over creation to renew and complete the work, to announce us 'innocent' once again.

There's no need to 'hide in the garden' for fear of the Father's reaction to our failings anymore. He is saying, 'If you're in trouble come to me first'. That's perfect love.

As we said previously, God's one purpose was to bring about the New Covenant. If I am driving to a clear and definable destination, to veer off to the left or to the right, or worse, to take a complete wrong turning, that will then be very difficult to reach that destination. Consistent disobedience of God's children led to so many consequences that are hard to swallow. Living in 21st century western culture is a world away from Middle Eastern BC culture, a very different way of life indeed! It is naive to read scripture from our own cultural and material perspective and think that we can just throw any light upon incidents where we make assumptions about God and his dealings with people.

Many tribes and nations worshipped gods like Molech who was only satisfied with devotees who would throw their children into fire, or whip them into walking into the fire to appease his evil nature. This was truly a satanic cult and as abhorrent to us as it was to God. It was of course obscene to the living God who loved his offspring, even the people of Israel being caught up in these types of practices and atrocities. Without repentance many paid the penalty and fell behind as a result. See Ez 16:21, 43.

If you'll excuse the irreverence, I was just thinking about an incidence in Pirates of the Caribbean where Jack Sparrow doesn't escape with the others back to the ship. It appears that he has 'fallen behind'. Considering whether to wait for him they decide, 'No, stick to the code, we go on!'. In a very small way perhaps that is a snapshot of some of the events of the Old Testament. The overriding and overwhelming plan of God was in the rescue mission of the Messiah, to redeem and save us from spiritual death, from the curse of the law and into the blessing of grace.

The theme that runs through the book of Hosea is one of redemption. The prophet is charged to marry the prostitute Gomer, even though she will not remain faithful to him, and even to 'buy her back' from her waywardness in order to demonstrate the love of God for his children. 'I will show love to the one I called Not My Loved One. I will say, "You are my people" to those who were called Not My People. And they will say, "You are my God"' (Hos 2:23b, NIRV). Only in the perfect love of the perfect Father can we be redeemed.

I remember as a young teenager, I used to spend a lot of time in my friends house, which was next door, because they had a T.V. We didn't. Eventually Dad decided to get one too. At least he could keep an eye or what I was watching that way. Unfortunately for Dad, at the same time as he bought the new black and white T.V. our neighbour upgraded to the super new colour! So I still went next door....

A far worse situation would be if your child decided to abandon you as their parent and go and live with another parent who seems more fun, especially if you knew that family was not all that they appeared to be. You might go to great lengths to restore your child to you and to confront those who would lead your child astray, and hold them to account. This is precisely what God is intent on accomplishing for us throughout the roadmap of the truth of the stories and prophecies of the Old Testament.

Outside of God's truth is falsehood. Outside of his blessing is the curse.

Outside of his purpose there is no future. Outside of his presence is loss.

Dress it up. Cover it with a veneer of hope and chase after every inviting promise that life can offer, but truly only the *offer of life*, given openly and freely by the Father, can ever satisfy the human condition and bring us into the freedom of how his creation was always intended to be – Perfect.

Of course in and of ourselves we cannot achieve this. Our good works won't do. Only in the *re-creation* of our hopeless position before our Lord and Saviour, can the curse be overthrown and we can be declared righteous, *made perfect* before Almighty God.

Chapter 3.

RUNNING AND RESCUE –
Covenant

A better way...

There really is nothing more exciting and fascinating than a voyage through the Old Testament. Amazing 'stand alone' stories that span the centuries, written by many authors with little or no connection, and yet linked together in purpose through prophecy and Holy Spirit inspired direction. Stand alone stories that actually stand together in foreshadowing the events to come.

In tracing our way through scripture, we are landing on characters and incidents of the greatest consequence, and by default we are also landing on covenants made with mankind by our Father God.

We will take a look at more of these covenants, they are important because the Love of God is the igniting spark to each one. So we'll make a bit of a 'drive through, whistle stop tour' of these covenants on our journey, as they are so integral and significant to knowing the Father's heart in a deeper way.

The Covenant That's Eternal: Before creation God covenanted with Jesus, eternal peace and redemption through his death and resurrection. (Heb 13:20; Eph 1:4)

Our Lord Jesus is the great Shepherd of the sheep. The God who gives peace brought him back from the dead. He did it because of the blood of the eternal covenant Heb 13:20. NIRV

God chose us to belong to Christ before the world was created. He chose us to be holy and without blame in his eyes. He loved us Eph 1:4. NIRV

David sums it up perfectly in Ps 139:13-16.

'For you created my inmost being; you knit me together in my mother's womb. I praise you because I am fearfully and wonderfully made; your works are wonderful, I know that full well. My frame was not hidden from you when I was made in the secret place, when I was woven together in the depths of the earth. Your eyes saw my unformed body; all the days ordained for me were written in your book before one of them came to be.'

<u>The Covenant In Eden</u>: In creation, God covenanted with man regarding care and dominion over the creation, with blessing that followed, together with relationship and parameters of obedience. (Gen 1: 26-28; Gen 2: 16-17)

Then God said, 'Let us make man in our image, after our likeness. And let them have dominion over the fish of the sea and over the birds of the heavens and over the livestock and over all the earth and over every creeping thing that creeps on the earth.'

So God created man in his own image, in the image of God he created him; male and female he created them.

And God blessed them. And God said to them, 'be fruitful and multiply and fill the earth and subdue it, and have dominion over the fish of the sea and over the birds of the heavens and over every living thing that moves on the earth.' Gen 1:26-28   ESV

The Lord God gave the man a command. He said, 'you can eat the fruit of any tree that is in the garden, but you must not eat the fruit of the tree of the knowledge of good and evil. If you do, you can be sure that you will die.' Gen 2:16-17   NIRV

This reveals the heart of the Father; to bless his children; to give them authority; to provide for them and walk daily with them.

<u>The Covenant To Adam:</u> Where the blessing and glory lifted, where the curse was introduced on Satan and upon the earth, where spiritual and physical death is the result, and yet a coming redeemer is promised. (Gen 3: 14-19)

The Lord God said to the serpent, 'Because you have done this, cursed are you above all livestock and above all the beasts of the field; on your belly you shall go, and dust you shall eat all the days of your life. I will put enmity between you and the woman, and between your offspring and her offspring; he shall bruise your head, and you shall bruise his heel.'

To the woman he said, 'I will surely multiply your pain in childbearing; in pain you shall bring forth children. Your desire shall be contrary to your husband, but he shall rule over you.'

And to Adam he said, 'Because you have listened to the voice of your wife and have eaten of the tree of which I commanded you, You shall not eat of it, cursed is the ground because of you; in pain you shall eat of it all the days of your life; thorns and thistles it shall bring forth for you; and you shall eat the plants of the field. By the sweat of your face you shall eat bread till you return to the ground, for out of it you were taken; for you are dust and to dust you shall return.' Gen 3: 14-19   ESV

It's a bitter pill to swallow. It seems like the antithesis of the previous covenant. The result of sin reverses the blessing of God, the curse of sin and death is let loose upon the earth and the authority given to man, is for a time taken by Satan.

<u>The Covenant With Noah</u>: Of government, accountability for ill treatment of living beings, promise of no destruction of the earth and blessing of fruitfulness and increase. (Gen 8: 20-9: 17)

'I will never again curse the ground because of man, for the intention of man's heart is evil from his youth. Neither will I ever again strike down every living creature as I have done.

While the earth remains, seedtime and harvest, cold and heat, summer and winter, day and night, shall not cease.'

And God blessed Noah and his sons and said to them, 'Be fruitful and multiply and fill the earth.' Gen 8: 21-9: 1   ESV

Demonic depravity brings ultimate judgement to mankind. But earth and mankind are replenished and renewed through one righteous man. Man is re-commissioned to be once more fruitful on the earth. In a dynamic change of all things, human life spans are reduced and destructive demonic powers are curtailed.

The Covenant For Abraham: Righteousness or right standing with God is credited to man by his faith. Blessing comes to all the nations on the earth, in him and settled through Christ. (Gen 12: 1-3; Gen 15: 1-21; Gal 3: 16-18)

Now the Lord said to Abram, 'Go from your country and your kindred and your Father's house to the land I will show you.

And I will make of you a great nation, and I will bless you and make your name great, so that you will be a blessing.

I will bless those who bless you, and him who dishonours you I will curse, and in you all the families of the earth shall be blessed.' Gen 12: 1-3   ESV

This significant covenant finds in Abram a man who is an alien to God, knows nothing about God, but is willing to know, willing to follow, and willing to set about being a Father to all peoples of the earth; called by God's name, through whom he can be both blessed, and become a blessing.

The Covenant Through Moses: Pertains to commandments, the law and transgression, social responsibility and reverence for God resulting in the coming of his glory. (Ex 20 - 24; 2 Cor 3: 7-11)

The old way, with laws etched in stone, led to death, though it began with such glory that the people of Israel could not bear to look at Moses' face. For his face shone with the glory of God, even though the brightness was already fading away. Shouldn't we expect far greater glory under the new way, now that the Holy Spirit is giving life? If the old way, which brings condemnation, was glorious, how much more glorious is the new way, which makes us right with God! In fact, that first glory was not glorious at all compared with the overwhelming glory of the new way. So if the old way, which has been replaced, was glorious, how much more glorious is the new, which remains forever! 2 Cor 3: 7-11   NLT

How do you control a nation of people who have lost their way, their hope and their desire? A rabble with no fixed abode or purpose. Find a Moses. 'Strong leadership is best served with warm heart!' Regulations are necessary, guidelines, law, social action and delegation. A God appointed and anointed leader is vital.

<u>The Covenant Of Life</u>: Offering of prosperity, restoration of fortune and compassion wherever this may occur, in following God in obedience, choosing life over death by speaking with the word of faith. (Deut 30: 1-20)

'I'm calling for the heavens and the earth to give witness against you this very day. I'm offering you the choice of life or death. You can choose either blessings or curses. But I want you to choose life. Then you and your children will live.

And you will love the Lord your God. You will obey him. You will remain true to him. The Lord is your very life. He will give you many years in the land. He promised to give that land to your fathers, to Abraham, Isaac and Jacob.' Deut 30: 19-20   NIRV

Also known as a 'Land Covenant' this is the most exhaustive and wonderful offer of life over death, blessing

over curse. Explicitly explained, openly offered and beautifully bestowed upon all who will turn and follow the Lord.

<u>The Covenant Speaking Promise</u>: This is the covenant made to David of promise that would be established eternally and become a greater permanent covenant for all man and for all time: The line, the throne and the kingdom. (2 Sam 7: 4-17; Luke 1: 31-33, Rev 5:5)

'Your house and your kingdom shall endure forever before me; your throne shall be established forever.' 2 Sam 7:16 NIV
'You will conceive and give birth to a son, and you are to call him Jesus.
He will be great and will be called the son of the most high. The Lord God will give him the throne of his Father David, and he will reign over Jacob's descendants for ever; his kingdom will never end.' Luke 1:31-33 NIV

Jesus was often referred to as 'Son of David.' These were those who recognised that Jeshua, Messiah, would be of the line of David, the very Son of man and Son of God. Those with eyes to see, and often the blind with no physical eyes to see, saw in Jesus the fulfilment of the promise. He is revealed by the Spirit. From the time of the covenant of David, 1000 years B.C. wise men were looking, waiting and anticipating...

<u>The Covenant Made New</u>: The new covenant is ratified through the redemption secured in Jesus. The blessing of this covenant is the culmination and completion of where all previous covenants pointed toward: It is unconditional,

unchanging, unending, unbroken and unbreakable. Final,
for us! (Jer 31:31-33; Heb 8: 8-12; Gal 3: 13-20)

'The days are coming', declares the Lord, 'when I will
make a new covenant with the people of Israel and with
the people of Judah. It will not be like the covenant
I made with their ancestors when I took them by the
hand to lead them out of Egypt, because they broke
my covenant, though I was a husband to them,' declares
the Lord.

'This is the covenant that I will make with the people of
Israel after that time,' declares the Lord. 'I will put my law
in their minds and write it on their hearts. I will be their
God, and they will be my people.' Jer 31:31-33 NIV

'For I will forgive their wickedness and will remember
their sins no more.' Heb 8:12 NIV

He redeemed us in order that the blessing given to
Abraham might come to the gentiles through Christ
Jesus, so that by faith we might receive the promise of the
spirit. Gal 3:14 NIV

And there's nothing Satan can do about it.
"It is finished!"

'Selah' is appropriate at this moment. Or, Hallelujah!
'Thank you oh my Father for giving us your son,
and leaving your spirit till the work in earth is done.'
(M. Green.)

So that was a bit of a 'fly-by' summation of Biblical
covenants. They are worth far more attention than I am
giving them here of course, but perhaps they will help us
in our understanding of the main purpose of this book.

If you have a mobile phone, you'll be used to regular updates. Sometimes they improve what was prior, other times they just seem to go a bit sideways and don't seem to really improve things greatly, if at all! It makes me think of successive covenants, with the final fulfilment of *everything* that has preceded it. The law, the prophets, the journey, all arrive at the cross. Jesus said: 'This cup is the new covenant in my blood, which is poured out for you' (Luke 22:20).

In the big stories of scripture we find where the major covenants are made. We looked briefly at Abraham in a previous chapter, although from another place, another belief and another history, he chose to believe God, relocate physically and spiritually and follow the heart of the Father who he did not yet know. He was the heir to the promise through whom we all benefit in that finished work of Jesus. He was even prepared to offer his son, his only son, the one heir of that promise in sacrifice at the word of God. Did he know that God would provide a ram? He knew in faith that God would make it right. He didn't know that God was showing us that he would 'make it right' for all people by unconditionally giving his own son in sacrifice. It's not easy is it to be uncomfortable and unconditional when we give back to God. Can we offer him everything? Do we really trust him to walk into the unknown even when we have the certainty to do so? Can we really believe that 'by his wounds we are healed?' It's pretty important that we can because 'without faith it is impossible to please God' (Heb 11:6). To 'please God' in this context doesn't infer that he just gets the hump if we aren't living and moving in faith. What it implies is that as we continue to grow in our trust of him above other things, *truly believing* that God is faithful to set us free, to deliver us, to heal and to prosper us, then that brings pleasure to God in answering our need. Faith is active, it activates in the spiritual dimension of our lives. It comes by the word. 'So then faith comes by hearing, and hearing by the word of God' (Rom 10:17, NKJV).

It is very true to say at this point that we have a common enemy who opposes all that our Lord has accomplished for us. The 'tenant' of this world is on the rampage perhaps more than ever in these last days, to rage against the covenant that the Father has made for us. 'Stay alert! Watch out for your great enemy, the devil. He prowls around like a roaring lion, looking for someone to devour' (1 Peter 5:8, NLT).

His desire is to destroy our faith. The Greek word here is *katapiein,* which means to swallow or to drown. But he is only *like* a roaring lion. The real Roaring Lion of the tribe of Judah has already won the argument, and we are secure in our position before God. Satan can only bring fear, despair, sickness, harmful incidents and the like, troublesome and destructive as they may be; but he cannot overcome the eternal destiny deposited in our spirit.

In the knowledge of this, how important it is to seek the covering of Heavenly Father in each and every circumstance of life, over every financial issue, over every medical condition and every demonic situation. Seek God before all other things and resist the devil. 'Stand firm against him, and be strong in your faith. Remember that your Christian brothers and sisters all over the world are going through the same kind of suffering that you are' (1 Peter 5:9, NLT).

The preceding verse in 1 Peter 5 prepares us in our stand against the enemy, and our focus on the provision, protection and purposes of the Lord for us. 'Casting all your cares (all your anxieties, all your worries, and all your concerns, once and for all) on Him, for He cares about you (with deepest affection, and watches over you very carefully') (1 Peter 5:7).

What a beautiful unpacking of this verse from the Amplified Bible. It teaches us that once we have rolled every care over unto the Lord, we are in a much stronger position to withstand the enemy. Faith and anxiety just don't work well together. They are like oil and water that wont mix. How important it is to run toward God before we run at the enemy, or from the enemy, to understand our covenant in the way that David understood his, when it came to facing his giants. (*See chapter 6*).

God has a consistent and constant rescue plan. When we run, he rescues. When we say 'no hope' he says 'covenant'. Our hope is in the promise. Hope never ends.

All the favour of God is upon us, like the stars in the sky or the sand on the seashore, God is searching for his covenant people to shower his love and blessing onto, healing, restoring, multiplying his faithfulness and bringing us joy in knowing him.

Chapter 4.

REBELLION AND REDEMPTION –
The Three Arks

In, through and over, but never *under* the circumstance

Ark#1

> But Noah found favour in the eyes of the Lord.
> (Gen 6:8)

> Make yourself an ark of gopher wood... (Gen 6:14)

Now Noah has a big story. He certainly ended up with one big boat!

In what is possibly the 'best known story' in the Bible, especially with children, we have a momentous situation in every sense of the word, and a story that is certainly not there *just* for the children.

The story of Noah occurs at a time when rebellion of mankind was at its height. Scripture tells us that 'the wickedness of man was great on the earth, and that every intent of the thoughts of his heart was only evil continually' (Gen 6: 1-13). We also learn here that the 'sons of God' were on the earth. These were probably the 'Nephelim' of whom we know little about, but many scholars would consider to be 'fallen angels': 'Naphal' in the Hebrew - 'to fall' - indicate that these beings were at the time corrupting mankind by bearing children with the 'daughters of men'. Further reference is found in Num 13:33, in the report of the inhabitants of Canaan.

Everything that was happening on earth was evil and satanic and would soon serve to destroy the creation in which mankind had been created to enjoy and to thrive. The plan of Satan is always to bring harm and to destroy. The plan of God is always to bring security and to create.

This is what we find at this moment of history. Here is a foretaste, a foreshadowing of what is to come through a *recreation* of the earth and the *redemption* of the sin of mankind.

God found Noah to be the one person whose heart had not been corrupted by the evil around him. He was righteous and blameless and walked with God.

I want to be like Noah. In all honesty, if I were the only believer with a heart for God, and I was surrounded by people who were totally against God and what I stood for, I know that I would find it tough to go against the grain and stay in His presence. For this, Noah found favour with God and was commissioned to build an ark of salvation for mankind. But 120 years? Now that is extraordinary. Ok, so we lived a lot longer back then. We had more time to get the job done. Maybe the pressures were different, but you still had to live for *today*, in real time. How could you tolerate ridicule and abuse for

120 years while you built a ship miles away from the sea. I would have packed it in after a year I'm sure. How can you stay faithful to God under such circumstances and preach repentance to those who thought that you were a joke?

I believe that only by the presence and the power of the Holy Spirit can you live by faith, facing and dealing with circumstances daily as they arrive. Noah lived his life daily, but with an eye on the purpose.

> Jesus said not to be anxious for the future. Tomorrow can be anxious for itself. 'Each day has enough trouble of its own.' Trust God daily, don't allow the enemy to disrupt what God has already done for you in Christ Jesus. Don't fuss and worry. Your Heavenly Father knows exactly what you need, so just seek him first and his righteousness. His job is to fulfil his blessing covenant with us. Ours is to store up treasure in heaven.   (Matt 6 abbr.)

Of course Noah hadn't seen the work of the Lord Jesus, but interestingly we read this in Hebrews 11:7. 'By faith Noah, when warned about things not yet seen, in holy fear built an ark to save his family. By his faith he condemned the world, and became heir of the righteousness that is in keeping with faith.'

There is strong indication here that Noah has seen what was to come. Perhaps it was a vision, maybe a visitation, but the word of God came to Noah and it was sufficient for the day and for everyday, something he was able to build his mission upon. David said in Psalm 119:105: 'Your word is lamp to my feet and a light to my path.' This path may be a rocky one but our walk with God is a daily walk and a daily trust. Seeing only a little step at a time can be frustrating. We want to see more of the picture, but then more could be truly scary! Trust God with the big things, he knows them all and how to lead us through the difficult waters, the troubled seas and darkest valleys, into safe, blessed and productive pastures.

Not only does the story of Noah and the ark of wood give us a picture of salvation, of spiritual recreation through the work of Jesus on a cross of wood, but it also points to a further completion of all things when there will be created a new heaven and earth, the ultimate destiny of the believer. The ark had one door and that door was open to any who would repent from their rebellion against God. Sadly no one took up the offer but that door stands open again through the open tomb and the resurrected Messiah. Never miss that opportunity.

There is something here also about household salvation. Noah brought his family into the security of the ark with him, as did Rahab in her home at the fall of Jericho. Though we need to all make individual commitments to God there is something important about bringing our families, our flesh and blood into the security of our faith in God, into our house of faith. God didn't want to destroy mankind in the flood. He wanted to destroy sin and its consequences. In praying for unrepentant spouses, children or parents, or other family members we are bringing them into the security of our individual 'ark'. We ultimately leave our loved ones in the hands of a sovereign and loving God, and righteous judge.

Ark#2

> But when she could no longer hide him, she took an
> ark of bulrushes for him, daubed it with asphalt and
> pitch, put the child in it and laid it in the reeds by
> the river's bank.   (Ex 2:3, NKJV)

From the huge and impressive gopher wood cruise ship, to the tiny and unimpressive bulrushes basket, we move to our second ark in the enormously significant story of Moses, how God brings redemption to a people enslaved by a power greater than they are able to free themselves from. Only God in his sovereignty can make a way through the wilderness when we feel trapped by circumstances beyond our control. We can use as many of our human resources as possible to find a way out but I know that sometimes life is like a maze, whichever path we try to take seems to lead to another dead end. Sometimes you pray and things get worse. I was at a conference in Brighton when John Wimber first came to the U.K. in the 1980's, and he would say that 'in the early days when the church started to believe in faith for healings and prayed for the sick, they just got sicker!'. But they pressed on because of the word of God and the promise. Then they saw the breakthrough. He doesn't leave and he doesn't forsake us.

Moses protests at the task given to him. 'What shall I say when they ask who sent me?' God simply replied: 'I Am Who I Am...I Am has sent me to you' (Ex 3:13b). Then to his own people God tells Moses to say: 'Yahweh, the God of your ancestors has sent me to you. This is my eternal name, my name to remember for all generations.' v.15. (NLT, *Para.*) God is the All Powerful Almighty God to the Egyptians, but is coming to his own people who are in desperate need, saying that he is *also* the personal God who can be trusted for all things and for all time. Yahweh or YHWH is usually rendered 'the Lord' as we read through the texts of scripture.

Things got significantly worse for the Israelites after Moses had gone to Pharaoh. How confusing that must have been after God had convinced Moses that he was for him, that nothing could come against him, despite his lack of self belief and his humanity, after all, God was divine and had promised.... 'Moses returned to the Lord and said, "O Lord, why have you brought trouble upon this people? Is this why you sent me? Ever since I went to Pharaoh to speak in your name, he has brought trouble upon this people, and you have not rescued your people at all"' (Ex 5:22-23).

God answers Moses in the following chapter that he is God Almighty; that he will deliver, he will remember the hardship because he will remember his covenant.

God also promises here that he would begin to reveal himself as the Lord, as Yahweh. Before this time he had always been Elohim, the strong, the powerful, the judge, and many derivatives of 'El' but here God is looking forward, here is such a powerful foretaste of future redemption, he is making himself known as more personal, more relational, more approachable. The name Elohim appears 2570 times, and Yahweh 6830 in the Hebrew text.[5] These numbers vary a little according to resources but can be approximated to around 2600 and 6800.

In Psalm 19, David describes the revelation of God to humanity through creation. In the first six verses he uses the title for God, El, then in verses 7-14 he moves to the more personal title for God in the Old Testament, the Lord. YHWH.

We are given a picture of how God reveals himself more intimately throughout scripture in a way that transforms our lives. In verse 7 David declares: 'The law of the Lord is perfect, refreshing the soul....' He closes in verse 14 by saying, 'May the words of my mouth and this meditation of my heart be pleasing in your sight, Lord my rock and my redeemer.'

Sometimes it seems, we need God to be the 'I Am' and at other times we need a 'Yahweh'. In Matt 14:27, in the boat, in the storm, the disciples cry out in fear and Jesus comes to them on the water saying 'don't worry, I Am is here' - The Almighty God has come to rescue. Then he reaches out to a drowning Peter and takes him in his arms and brings him to safety. He is Yahweh, in person. The redeemer. Relax. Immanuel has come - God with us.

He is Sovereign over all of his creation. Interestingly, the word 'Sovereign' of which we are very familiar doesn't appear in all translations of the Bible. Especially the earlier ones, but perhaps if we are able to take our 'Elohim' and our 'Yahweh' and combine these to be the inseparable nature of God, we can understand and trust him in being the Almighty and All loving Father that he is. 'Sovereign over us.' That is not to say that the supreme ruler of the universe exercises a kind of control over us that we dare not challenge. His perfect love negates that theory. We have already seen how Abraham appealed to God on behalf of his family, and we know that he is 'moved by prayer'. The apostle Paul says:

'Rejoice always, pray continually, give thanks in all circumstances; for this is God's will for you in Christ Jesus' (1 Thess 5:16-18).

'The prayer of a righteous person is powerful and effective' (James 5:16b).

God is most certainly not a dictator. He rejoices in living in partnership with us.

Salvation came for the people in going through the waters. Whereas Noah rode above the water, Moses would lead through the water. Redemption comes because God is both above and below every human circumstance. He is there to undergird and oversee our faith, to bring us freedom and deliverance.

I don't know about you but I still often find myself leaning toward rebellion. Like the leaning tower of Pisa I seem to be naturally inclined that way! I want to go my way, it seems a little easier or it makes more sense to go in my direction. Forgetting that God is sovereign, I plough on and then find that the harvest wasn't down that way after all. It happened to the Israelites and in their grumbling saw 40 years of wandering in the desert. How did Moses cope with that, 40 years in the waiting in no mans land, waiting for a word from God, and then just short of the finish line, another 40 years with this crowd! No wonder he got angry, frustrated and exhausted! Do you remember how in a temper Moses struck the rock as he had done previously instead of speaking to it as God had asked? (Num.20). He wasn't without sin or disobedience, neither are we. Jumping ahead of God really isn't what he is looking for, and will scarcely aid us on our journey. Presume that he knows the better way. Don't 'assume' that you do.

What made the difference for Moses, how did he relate to God in a deeper and more powerful way than any before him or after him? One clue is in chapter 12 of Exodus. Aaron and Miriam were doing some assuming themselves. Miriam spoke against Moses, in essence saying 'what's so special about him?' - the big green giant was showing its face, but verse 3 is highlighted: 'Now Moses was a very humble man, more humble than any other man on the face of the earth.'

That is so telling. In humility or reverence before God, there is a lifting up into the very presence of God. James 4:10 says, 'Humble yourselves before the Lord and he will lift you up.'

(1 Peter 5:6): 'Humble yourselves therefore under God's mighty hand that he may lift you up in due time.'

(Phil 2:8): 'And being found in appearance as a man, he humbled himself and became obedient to death - even death on a cross.' Jesus was lifted up, first on the cross, then from the grave in glory, and into heaven where he has all authority.

So why do we grumble, and why do we moan? We aren't promised a smooth ride through life. When the Lord called Paul he said that he would show him how much he would suffer for his namesake. We are in a battle against principalities and powers, against a fallen world, sometimes against ourselves but also at times, knowingly or unknowingly, against God himself. Remember: 'He is for us, not against us.'

We looked briefly at this in the first chapter but it's worth revisiting.

You can't separate God's glory from his goodness. Exodus 33 gives us a slight dilemma in telling us that 'the Lord would speak to Moses face to face, as one speaks to a friend.' Later on Moses asks to see God's glory and God replies that he cannot see his face and live. Verse 11 is most likely to mean a relationship that is intimate, being expressed by the words 'face to face'. God is a Spirit and can only be seen through the incarnate Jesus. God says in verse 19: 'I will cause all my goodness pass in front of you.' In verses 22-23: 'When my glory passes by, I will put you in the cleft in the rock and cover you with my hand until I have passed by. Then I will remove my hand and you will see my back, but my face must not be seen.'

God's goodness or his love is inseparable from his glory. This is a beautiful scripture because it shows God hiding us in a safe place with his hand of protection and then revealing the intent of his goodness, the nature of the character of his glory.

Thomas R Schreiner writes: 'Since God is King and Lord, it is his purpose and design that he be glorified in all things and by all people. Some have complained that such a God is narcissistic, but that objective misses the point. For God as King glorifies himself by giving himself to his human beings in love. God is honoured as King when human beings receive and depend upon his love and experience his salvation. God's glory and God's love must not be placed into two separate compartments. Rather, God is glorified as Lord in his love for human beings. The sovereignty of God and his Kingship take place in history, in the story recounted in the scriptures, revealed supremely in the ministry and person of Jesus Christ.'[6]

Summarising our brief visit to such a momentous time, we can view this story unmistakably as the reconciliation of all mankind to a redemptive God. The infant Moses escapes the slaughter of all the other infants, to grow up in an alien household in order to deliver God's people, and bring them from captivity and into freedom. Under the purpose and protection of a loving Father there is clearly a projection, a foreshadowing of the coming King, Jesus our saviour who escapes another slaughter to be an alien in our world, the mediator of not only the chosen people of the Old Covenant, but of *all* peoples through the coming of the New Covenant.

Ark#3

Let them make an ark of acacia wood... (Ex 25:10)

The much sought after Ark of the Covenant. The mystery of the ages and the stuff of Hollywood movies!

In Exodus 25:10-22, Moses is given instructions to make the Ark of the Covenant. This would become a place where God in his divinity could meet with man in his humanity through the high priest. It was the only place of atonement for sins, and as such foreshadows Jesus who brings a permanent atonement, both past and future. Jesus of course replaces the ark in this sense, being the only way of salvation by his sacrifice on the cross.

There on the lid would be the solid gold atonement cover with the two cherubim or angels facing one another. God spoke to Moses: 'There, above the cover between the two cherubim that are over the ark of the Testimony, I will meet with you and give you all my commands for the Israelites' (Ex 25: 22).

Within the ark was to be the Ten Commandments, a pot of manna and the rod of Aaron. They were there to represent the law, the essence of the holiness of God, his love and care and provision in the manna and the eternal priesthood from Aaron to Jesus, our great High Priest. The ark would be a symbol of God's presence and protection and also once a year a place where there could be atonement for sins.

A way of looking at atonement in the Bible is that in the Old Testament it was essentially to cover, in the New Testament atonement speaks of remittance of sins.

Today we can look at our sins and our failures as no longer simply under cover, but cancelled and forgotten in remittance through our repentance. The law that stood against us has been atoned for by grace. The 'mercy seat' on the ark has become a mercy seat in us by the indwelling presence of the Holy Spirit.

You can approach God anytime and anywhere. The curtain that separated God from man was torn down at the cross. Don't run from the Father. If you've been in rebellion against what you might have thought of as the law of God, or the God of law, it's time to take a walk in redemption, to run to the Father, run to the love of God. As David said: 'Taste and see that the Lord is good, blessed is the one who takes refuge in him' (Ps 34:8).

You know, we can be in rebellion against God as believers in more ways than one. We tend to think of rebellion as just 'turning away from God', but when we are told that it's by faith that we move the hand of God, yet rely on our own abilities, or trust in the circumstances around us, or in other people, we are really acting in rebellion. If we speak against a brother or a sister we are acting against God's purpose. See James 4:11-12. If we speak negatively we are still under the law and not under grace, we are activating the curse and not the blessing.

We've been reconciled to our Heavenly Father but it's important to daily walk in that reconciliation.

'For we do not have a high priest who is unable to sympathise with our weaknesses, but one who in every respect has been tempted as we are, yet without sin. Let us then with confidence draw near to the throne of grace, that we may receive mercy and find grace to help in time of need' (Heb 4:15-16, ESV).

Hebrews 10:22-23 tells us to, 'let us draw near with a true heart in full assurance of faith, with our hearts sprinkled clean from an evil conscience and our bodies washed with pure water. Let us hold fast the confession of our hope without wavering, for he who promised is faithful' (ESV).

I could suggest here that there is a fourth ark, or many more arks. Not only did God travel in the arks with Noah and Moses, he travelled in the ark of the Old Covenant and now travels in the ark of the New Covenant, within us, by his Spirit. We have become his ark, the carrier on display of his blessing, his presence and his purpose, in redeeming all who would come. Hold fast, don't give in and don't give way to the enemy of our faith that is given freely by the love of God and the blood of Jesus.

'Therefore do not throw away your confidence, which has a great reward. For you have need of endurance, so that when you have done the will of God you may receive what is promised' (Heb 10: 35-36, ESV).

Chapter 5.

BLESSING AND BELONGING –
Carry His Presence

A little incident with a big consequence…

So here we come upon one of those troublesome incidents that we find scattered across the pages of scripture. While we are on the subject of the Ark of the Covenant, it's worth taking some time to have a look at the story of Uzzah from 2 Samuel 6, and again in 1 Chronicles 13. It's a challenging story, particularly at first sitting and requires some attention to the detail and insight into the 'back story'. Things can't always be taken at face value, that's as true in the circumstances of life as it is in the interpretation of the difficult passages in the Bible.

20 years ago when we lived in Eastbourne a new neighbour moved in opposite. No one in the close liked him as he was loud and often in trouble with the law. I wanted to be friendly toward him and one day he caught me outside and offered me a very large block of cheese for £10. My immediate inclination was to decline the offer; the dubious acquisition and the cholesterol were not too appealing! However, whilst observing the cheese in one hand I completely missed the rather large knife in

the other hand, which was not there just to cut the cheese, but to prompt me in a different direction. Suddenly I was overwhelmed with a new desire for cheddar and quickly parted with said £10!

This story of Uzzah in the Old Testament I have struggled with. It has been a puzzle to me, it was a puzzle to David and perhaps it's a puzzle for you too. In 2 Sam 6, Uzzah appears to give God a 'helping hand' with good intentions, in steadying the moving of the Ark to Jerusalem after making all the arrangements and ends up dead as a result.

David is too confused, angry and scared to take the Ark further, so he leaves it in the house of a chap called Obed-Edom for three months, whom becomes blessed by having the presence of God living with him. One is seemingly cursed whilst the other is blessed. Why should this be? Well, a little background is helpful here.

God gave specifics over the care of the Ark. Firstly only priests could approach the Ark, and that after offering sacrifices, Lev 16. Secondly, the Ark must be lifted with acacia poles, not with hands, but by being carried on shoulders to its destination, not plonked onto a cart whether new or old. Thirdly, the Ark was to be carried by Koathite priests of whom Uzzah was a descendant and should have been aware of the 'terms and conditions'. Sadly he ignored the 'makers instructions' and paid the consequences of his poor judgement.

Starting Over...

If like me, you have ever put together some flat pack furniture, you may have read the instructions and followed them so far, before going your own way thinking that you have it all covered. Then you hit a problem because you didn't keep referring to the manual, and then have to undo some of it and start again where you went wrong.

That can happen a lot with us spiritually. We just tend to go it alone, forgetting that it's so much better when we simply rely on the direction that the Lord is guiding us and leading us in. Then it's 'back track time' to start over from where we left God behind....

As for our story, God's presence actually always intends to bring a blessing and not a curse and this is demonstrated in the life of Obed-Edom. After 3 months David sees how the household of Obed-Edom is blessed and returns to bring the Ark to Jerusalem and move it according to the makers instructions, including reverence, sacrifice and much joy! Three really important ingredients if we want to enjoy the full blessing of God in our lives.

The problem is, we often get angry or fearful over situations that we don't fully understand in our lives. When things get too tough, and God seems absent and no longer 'for us', it's time to remember his promise 'never to leave us or forsake us' (Deut 31: 6). Begin to reverence his name, take time to seek him afresh and let the joy of the Lord be your strength.

'Behold, God is my salvation; I will trust, and will not be afraid; for the Lord God is my strength and song, and he has become my salvation. With joy you will draw water from the wells of salvation. And you will say in that day: Give thanks to the Lord, call upon his name, make known his deeds among the peoples, proclaim that his name is exalted. Sing praises to the Lord, for he

has done gloriously; let this be known in all the earth'
(Isa 12: 2-5, ESV).

The name Obed means 'serve' or 'worship' and was a
name we see in a few accounts listed in scripture.
We don't know much about Obed-Edom, but David
knew enough to believe that he could trust the Ark
with him, and at that moment didn't seem to be sure
that he could trust himself further. After David had later
removed the ark to Jerusalem, Obed-Edom pops up in
a few references, as a gatekeeper, a housekeeper and a
worship leader before God, so pretty much living up to
his name!

It would appear that if this was the same Obed-Edom,
he would make sure he and his family went with the Ark.
After being blessed he wasn't about to go back to his old
life. He wanted to stay under the anointing in continued
blessing, and to *be* a blessing.

His attitude was very similar in this sense to Jabez of
whom we also have little reference. In 1 Chronicles 4:9
we read that 'Jabez was more honourable than his
brothers.'

His prayer was: '"Oh that you would bless me indeed,
and enlarge my territory, that your hand would be with
me, and that you would keep me from evil, that I may
not cause pain." So God granted him what he requested'
(1 Chron 4: 10, NKJV).

You can find Jabez in a list of the descendants of
Judah, whom are named but nothing is known. When we
get to Jabez however, the writer pauses and gives us that
little gem of information about him. He is clearly worthy
of note for us to be told that although his name means
that he 'was born in pain', he was determined to overcome

the troubles of the past and press into God and all that he had for him. This is true humility and perseverance.

There is something revealing about the character of these Old Testament figures that we need to emulate. There is a sense of a heart running after God, a determination to be blessed and to be a blessing through belonging, knowing that you *truly* belong to God and his family.

When it came to my not so friendly neighbour, at first I only noticed the helpful hand, not the one that showed his character and motive, which wasn't so pure after all.

With Uzzah, all seems well on the surface, even generous in his actions but he has taken the presence of God for granted, not acted humbly, wisely or worshipfully, but in presumption.

In *Raiders of the lost Ark,* the Nazis seek the Ark for their own gain and all die as they open it in their attempts to harness the power of God. Indiana says 'close your eyes, don't look at it' - perhaps a reference to when God said to Moses, 'no one can see God and live'. The Nazis in pride and arrogance all die while Indy and friend in supposed humility and deference are spared. It's a fanciful story but with a significant message.

We all have 'why' questions to things that we don't understand. The certainty that we have is that God wants to bless us, his children, and not to harm us, to give us a hope and a future. (Jer 29:11, *Para.*)

What we don't want to do is to take his presence for granted. His presence with us is a costly one. It cost him everything. It costs us so little in comparison.

I think that it's worth concluding this chapter with our own 'prayer of Jabez.'

'We thank you Father that we belong to you. As with the Ark of the Covenant we want to carry your presence daily and not just assume it.

We want to carry your presence internally and externally and without complacency, to seek you and find you when we seek you with all of our heart. Help us to remain humble before you, with wisdom in our life choices and worshipful in all our deeds, that we might be both blessed and a blessing.'

Chapter 6.

SIN AND SANCTIFICATION –

'We Three Kings'

(Of Israel are...)

There were three Kings of Israel initially, before the Kingdom split into two: Israel in the North and Judah in the South. The 'Kings' were firstly: King Saul, followed by King David, and succeeded by his son, King Solomon.

The stories that accompany the lives of each are most revealing in how we relate to God, how we deal with failure or success and how we overcome times of pressure or stress that regularly come our way.

The sad truth about sin is that it brings separation from God. Salvation however brings *sanctification* from God. These elements were all evident in our three cases that we are looking at in this chapter.

King#1

> Do you see the man the Lord has chosen?
> There is no one like him among all the people.
> (1 Sam 10: 24)

Saul was the ideal King. He came from a respected clan and had a father who was also well respected. He was head and shoulders taller than anyone else, handsome and looked noble. He was 30 years old when he became King, the same age as Jesus, when he was anointed for his ministry. He was of the age when careers began, of anointing for new beginnings. He represented Kingship and appeared to be the perfect choice. What could possibly go wrong?

The problem I believe with Saul is that he just wasn't ready for the task set before him. He hadn't experienced the wilderness years where his heart would be tested and proved. A few years later the wilderness years would become the honing and growing ground for David, but the withering and dying ground for Saul. Just as for David, the wilderness for Jesus also became that victorious 'proving' ground. Following the anointing of the Spirit upon his life came that vital strength to experience death and resurrection, and his ultimate triumph over the destructive sin of pride in the plans of the enemy.

With King Saul, sadly he soon began to believe that 'he was the man' - irreproachable.

After what seemed like a nervous start he appeared to assume his role honourably. However, as he began to 'curry favour' with the people, he was unfortunately unable to walk in humility for any length of time. Without humility it could only be a matter of time before insecurities and character flaws would out, and that can be seen after the Goliath incident, when more praise was heaped upon David than was coming Saul's way. 'Saul has slain his thousands and David his tens of thousands. Saul was very angry...and from that time on Saul kept a close [jealous] eye on David' (1 Sam 18: 7-9).

Celebrity status had become the priority for Saul and self- indulgence only leads a person in one direction and it's not a direction that you want to travel in. In only 2 years as a King, Saul has been grossly disobedient by taking on the priestly role of offering sacrifices in 1 Sam 13. He pretty much ignored the rebuke of Samuel, and it didn't appear to truly affect Saul that he would lose the kingdom and another would be chosen.

What is interesting here is that Saul actually reigned as King for around 42 years. He was only 2 years in at this point and he was going to hang on in as long as he could, which may remind us of some of the dictators of our day - and the odd politician....

There were still moments of success, times of anointing upon Saul even, but he really began to spiral downward when David came on the scene. His ambition to hunt down God's chosen replacement overwhelmed every fibre of his being, and the kingdom was overlooked in his heart of revenge and hatred toward David.

At this point, the anointing from God had moved from Saul to David. His purpose would be fulfilled through David, yet the process of that coming to pass would be a long, difficult and painful journey for David.

It can sometimes seem an awful long time for answers to prayer, prayers that we believe have been answered, but the fulfilment still not realised. Waiting in the wilderness, weeks, months or years can be challenging, or even make us desperate at times as we search for God and his loving kindness, but of this we can learn so much from the shepherd and the King, David.

There are two destinations that sin leads to. There is the unrepentant and unresolved sin that ultimately leads to total failure, rejection and death, and there is the sin that is repented of, that is resolved and which leads to salvation, acceptance, and life.

As far as separation goes, there is therefore sin that leads to complete separation from God, but as believers there is also sin that leads to an *estrangement* from God. When we walk in the flesh, when we forget to acknowledge God, when we omit to include him in the details of life, and when we say, 'I can take it from here', we begin to lose the presence, the 'closeness' of God, because although he is almighty, he is also humble, as Jesus ultimately demonstrated in the atonement of sin on the cross. In all this, The Holy Spirit is continually working within us to iron out the creases, to show us more of God's character of love and kindness, that we might better represent his glory.

The further that Saul took the route that he did, the lower he sank and the more he represented the devil. Remember what Satan said in Isaiah 14: 'I will ascend above...I will set my throne on high...I will sit on the mount...I will ascend above the heights...I will make myself like the most high.' Isaiah writes, 'But you are brought down to the lowest...' *(Para)*.

As we looked at previously, to be humble is to be lifted or raised up. If anyone knew Jesus personally it was Peter, who himself wrote: 'God opposes the proud but shows favour to the humble. Humble yourselves, therefore, under

God's mighty hand, that he may lift you up in due time. Cast all your anxiety on him, because he cares for you' (1 Peter 5: 5b-7).

The root of the word 'opposes' essentially implies to be 'batting for the other team'. So God is seen here as turning round and standing against pride. He has to because of his perfect character. He opposes that which would exalt itself as higher than him because he knows that 'pride goes before destruction and a haughty spirit before a fall' (Proverbs 16:18).

Humility leads us into God's presence. In humility we carry his presence, just as Mary was chosen to literally 'carry the Son of God'. In her song of praise she says, "My soul magnifies the Lord, and my spirit has rejoiced in God my Saviour. For he has regarded the lowly state of his maidservant; For behold, henceforth all generations will call me blessed. For he who is mighty has done great things for me, and holy is his name" (Luke 1: 46-49, NKJV).

If you are on a journey that is leading you out of his presence, if troubles have come your way and you are trying to work it all through in your own strength and not in the spirit, then it's time to seek God afresh, bring him back on the scene, back into first place, perhaps you are still waiting, maybe things still aren't all coming together, but cast those anxieties over on to him and in 'the proper time', in his time, he will lift you up.

King Saul's times of repentance were few and not purposeful. He asked David for forgiveness and then continued his path of murderous jealousy and anger. Be purposeful in pursuit of God. Make a strong decision that God knows just what you need and trust him to work his purposes out. 'As pride brings destruction so humility brings honour' (Pro 18:12). It is all too easy to be inconsistent in our walk with God and fall back on our own abilities, but we have been made to stand upon his grace and his favour and to run with his ability. Live the truth of the scripture that says, ...'you have been raised with Christ... Set your mind on things above, not on earthly things' (Col 3:1-2).

Say it purposefully as Mary did in Luke 1:38: 'Be it unto me according to your word' (KJV).

King#2

> Rise up and anoint him. From that day on,
> the Spirit of the Lord came upon David in power.
> (1 Sam 16:12-13, abbr.)

Walking in the anointing makes all the difference. Walking outside of the anointing of God will often lead to heartache, depression and despair as it did with Saul.

Many times in the gospels Jesus is referred to as 'the son of David'. In Matt 1, right at the beginning of the New Testament we read: 'The book of the genealogy of Jesus Christ, the son of David, the son of Abraham.'

Jesus was often called 'Jesus, son of David' - particularly by those who recognised who he was through miracles, healing and teaching. There was a recognition of 'the Messiah who has come amongst us'. He was anointed for Kingship as David was anointed, and appointed to die and be raised again in order that his anointing can be upon all believers.

There was something so special, so powerful about the way that David 'did life' that it would be fully understood that the Messiah would be in his line. As God would be a Heavenly Father, so David would be as a spiritual, earthly Father.

To walk in that anointing is so vital for us as we seek to know and follow the will of the Father, day by day.

The story of the shepherd King David is so huge, we can't possibly do justice to it in this book. There are plenty of authors who have made a far better and more comprehensive job of teaching us about David than I could attempt to do, but here we are particularly engaging in David's life with reference to Sin, Salvation and Sanctification.

The very first thing that we learn about David is that his heart was always toward God. He always leant that way. As a shepherd boy, whom he may well have been when he wrote Psalm 23, he saw the shepherding that God did over him and how that related to his shepherding of the sheep. He knew intuitively that as sheep need a shepherd, so did he, so do we; to lead us through rough pastures, dark valleys, troublesome times, into places of rest, beside still waters, where *He* is, leading, restoring and disciplining.

We'll come back to this Psalm later in our summary of the purpose of this journey.

David had been in the presence of God in a serious way. At the sight of Goliath his hackles were up. He was ready for battle, ready to serve, ready to defend the name of the Lord, and ready to give his own life if need be in seeing God honoured. Can we go that far? I honestly don't know if I can, but I also want to lean that way.

When our Goliath comes - the big 'impossibles', the redundancy, the unpayable bills, the family loss, the relationship problems, the sickness and the terminal diagnosis - can we really be like David? Can we run at the goliaths under the authority of the anointing and shout - 'I come against you in the name of the Lord Almighty' (1Sam 17:45b).

The enemy comes against us with the sword and the spear, he uses the weapons that he knows he can use, but the weapons of our warfare are spiritual. They are given for us to use, because 'If God is for us, who can be against us? He who did not spare his own Son, but gave him up for us all, how will he not also, along with him, graciously give us all things?' (Rom 8:31).

We can only accomplish this by digging deeper into the promises of the Father, of remembering how many times God has been there for us, has rescued us, maybe in ways we didn't expect or in a timing that seemed all wrong and then fell into place as we look back. David looked back and he saw God rescuing him from the lion and the bear. That was all the fire he needed to ignite his faith and believe that he would receive what was promised.

'Who shall separate us from the love of Christ? Shall trouble or hardship or persecution or famine or nakedness or danger or sword? As it is written: For your sake we face death all day long; we are considered as sheep to be slaughtered (Ps 44:22). No, in all these things we are more than conquerors through him who loved us. For I am convinced that neither death nor life, neither angels or demons, neither the present or the future, nor any powers, neither height nor depth, nor anything else in all creation, will be able to separate us from the love of God that is in Christ Jesus our Lord' (Rom 8:35-39).

The beautiful thing about David is that although he didn't walk in victory continually, in fact things weren't working out well at all, anointed as King but no throne in sight, chased constantly by Saul, years of wilderness wandering with no immediate or easy answers, still his life remained a testimony of a man who kept his heart pure and humble toward the Lord. 'I will bless the Lord at all times, his praise shall continually be in my mouth' (Ps 34:1). 'I sought the Lord, and he heard me, and delivered me from all my fears' (Ps 34:4). These are purposeful and intentional words of David in one of his many times of trouble.

Despite falling into sin of the most terrible type, of adultery and murder, he knew to run to God in repentance and not run from him. In Psalm 51, David acknowledges God's mercy, his sin that stands between them, the evil he has done; that he was born in sin and that he needs to be forgiven, cleansed and restored, that his sins need to be blotted out and a new spirit be renewed within him. Here in verse 11 he pleads that God would not cast him away, that he would not lose his presence. He is still desperate to have the presence of God go with him, and he is broken and humble before the Lord, v17.

It is the sin that brings separation, but in the *nearness* of God's presence, not in the position of eternal salvation. Always keep a short account with God like David did, it's so important to stay in the anointing. There were consequences for David that were tough to endure, but you know, the consequences of our sin were upon Jesus.

He bore the penalty. How much more should we run to God in our failure, and not to despise what Jesus has accomplished. 'It would be like crucifying the Son of God all over again and subjecting him to public disgrace' (Heb 6:6, *Para*).

You see, in a true scriptural sense, whereas we ditch the thought of the law in favour of grace as its opposite, it is in fact lawlessness that is the opposite of law, and of grace it is disgrace. To be put to death on a cross would have been seen as bringing disgrace upon a person and his name. Jesus became a curse for us so that we could experience salvation and our name be engraved upon the palm of his hands. 'Christ is the culmination of the law so that there may be righteousness for everyone who believes' (Rom 10:4).

David didn't know Jesus in his humanity, and yet with all that we know of Jesus now, David instinctively sensed was there, present in the Father 1000 years before the birth of the Messiah. He never met the person of Jesus, and yet he prophesied of his coming, his death and resurrection. There are many references of the coming of the Messiah throughout the Psalms. David's words in Ps 22 for example make a clear prophetic statement regarding the death of Christ on the cross.

Perhaps he couldn't love Jesus as we love and relate to Jesus, but he loved the Father, and the law of God, because *there,* Jesus is represented in the Father's perfect character. He explores his relationship with the Father and the Law in Ps 119:7-16 (and throughout the Psalm), to praise God with an upright heart, to remain pure, seek him, live by his word, to hide his word in his heart that he might not sin against him, to speak the word, rejoice, meditate and delight in his ways and not neglect him.

'Oh, how I love your law! I meditate on it all day long' (Ps 119:97).

For David, the law brought freedom, which may be the opposite of how we have perceived it. 'I will always obey your law forever and ever. I will walk about in freedom for I have sought out your precepts' (Ps 119:44-45).

We look at the law and are so grateful of grace. David looked at the law and was so grateful for mercy. He knew what he didn't deserve and that was the underlying motivation of his heart.

A look back to Uzzah here and perhaps it's not; why should God let Uzzah die, but why should God let us live?

David knew first hand of God's salvation. He saw it time and again, he lived it and experienced it, he taught it, he gave it away to others, and he knew the discipline that accompanied walking in salvation. 'His mercies are new every morning.' It was a daily walk for David as it is for us. For us, salvation brings sanctification. Becoming more like him is God's intent for us. Living in love, by faith, obedient to his word, walking in the presence of the Holy Spirit and enjoying his blessing. Allowing the Holy Spirit to access those areas that we feel we can't approach God with, becomes actually how to *truly* draw close to him and know his kindness and compassion at such a deeper and more wonderful level.

As David shepherded his sheep and then the Kingdom, so God seeks to shepherd us, his people, that his goodness and mercy will follow us all the days of our life.

King#3

> But I am only a little child...So give your servant a
> discerning heart to govern your people and to
> distinguish between right and wrong. (1 Kings 3:7-9)

Solomon was born into privilege. Being raised and mentored by David his own father, and witnessing the successes and the failures of his Kingship, he faced a choice.

Does he lean back on the reputation and skills of his father and live in the benefit of that, or does he start afresh, be his own man, and recognise that he too has to walk with God, and develop his own personal relationship.

He makes an excellent decision. He comes before God, and in all the enormity of what life will throw at him; he comes as 'a little child'. That's impressive, whatever comes our way; there is no better position than to come as a child to God in total trust. Remember what Jesus said when the disciples were trying to scurry the children away: '...Let the children come to me. Don't stop them! For the kingdom of heaven belongs to those who are like these children' (Matt 19:14, NLT).

Children often come with a trust and an expectancy that is simple and innocent. We on the other hand as adults learn distrust and how to question. The Father would love us to come to him with the former - The simple trust of faith and expectancy.

Solomon puts God first in his actions. Before going on to build his own home, he builds a home for God. He spares no expense, or time in the construction of the first temple for God. He wants to do something extraordinary for

God before he looks to his own needs and desires. So often have I wanted to get my 'house' just perfect before I look to see what God is actually asking me for: My house here can be my job, my family, my entertainment, my enjoyment of music or sport, my holidays, _me, my and myself_. The unholy trinity!

The beauty of putting God first for Solomon was that God would add all those things when he chose to walk in integrity and humility. In fact so much blessing came upon him that he became the wisest, most respected and wealthiest man on earth. When the Queen of Sheba comes to check it out for herself, she pretty much says, 'You gotta be kidding me!' (1 Kings 10 paraphrased.) When she sees the blessing, God's favour, she declares: 'praise be to the Lord your God, who has delighted in you and placed you on the throne of Israel' (1 Kings 10:9).

I don't know about you but I think that the Father would love it if we walked so close to him that the glory of his character would shine out from us, that unbelievers would say - I want what they have. When we walk in his presence it shows, it's a reflection of God's glory, his loving kindness, just as Moses experienced on the mountain, he radiated the glory.

King Solomon wrote the 'Song of Solomon' or Song of Songs' the most intimate book of the Bible speaking of deep love, of human sexual love but with an underlying sense of the depth of the spiritual relationship that is between us, and God.

He wrote 3000 proverbs and 1000 songs. Probably he also wrote Ecclesiastes. I would say that he had a pretty good work ethic and that his words of wisdom from God speak to all people in all generations.

Sadly his incredible wealth and fame overcame his hunger for God. His many wives turned his heart toward other gods, on to other things and he fell into the dangerous trap of the lust of the flesh. In the book of Ecclesiastes, Solomon records his journey of life. Maybe they're his memoirs? He records the futility of life. A life spent in pursuing self doesn't bring peace. Fulfilment and joy go missing. In the last chapter, he records, 'Remember your creator in the days of your youth, before the days of trouble come and the years approach when you will say, I find no pleasure in them' (Eccl 12:1).

Remember *him* otherwise it's 'all meaningless....'

Whereas David experienced and welcomed the discipline of God in his life, Solomon forgot about that in his desire to live the good life.

It's a nice easy option to 'settle' as we get older in age, or older in faith, especially when still looking for promises to be fulfilled. Paul says in Phil 3:12, that although he hasn't arrived at his goal, he would press on to take hold of that for which Christ Jesus took hold of him. You can never stop learning about God the Father this side of eternity, and he will never stop encouraging you to 'continue to work out your salvation with fear and trembling, for it is God who works in you to will and act in order to fulfil his good purpose' (Phil 2:12b-13).

Welcome the work of sanctification by the Holy Spirit in your heart today, because he is making you more like him, perfect, loving and kind.

Saul started with good intentions, briefly, but unfortunately he finished very badly, separated from God, refusing discipline and losing the promise of the kingdom.

David started very well and finished very well, knew salvation, accepting discipline and receiving the promise of the kingdom and the kingdom to come.

Solomon started well but finished poorly. He also knew salvation, but turned away from God and knew the separation of his intimate presence and the Kingdom.

We could also refer to three Kings of Judah: Ahaz, who was terrible from start to finish, his son Hezekiah who began and ended so well that '...there was no-one like him among all the Kings of Judah', and his son Manasseh, who sadly undid all the good of his father in the most appalling ways, but importantly *repented* of his sin - and finished well.

What we take from this is that no matter the journey, like the repentant thief on the cross, the important message here is that we endeavour to finish our journeys well.

Where do we stand on our journey? Do we remain in sin? Have we experienced the work of salvation in us? How do we deal with his sanctifying work within us? Like the thief and Manasseh, we must humbly turn toward the Lord in surrender. He longs to establish his image in us, so that we can enjoy him and live in his eternal blessings.

John tells us to reject the love of the world, of things that draw us away from God.

'Do not love the world or anything in the world. If anyone loves the world, love for the Father is not in them. For everything in the world - the lust of the flesh, the lust of the eyes, and the pride of life - comes not from the Father but from the world. The world and its desires pass away, but whoever does the will of God lives forever' (1 John 2:15-17).

In conclusion of this section of 'Embracing the Father'- we find these remarkable words of the Apostle John as he writes his first letter.

Dear friends, let us love one another, for love comes from God. Everyone who loves has been born of God and knows God. Whoever does not love does not know God, because God is love. This is how God showed his love among us: he sent his one and only Son into the world that we might live through him. This is love: not that we loved God, but he loved us and sent his Son as an atoning sacrifice for our sins. Dear friends, since God so loved us, we also ought to love one another, God lives in us and his love is made complete in us. This is how we know that we live in him and he in us: he has given us of his Spirit. And we have seen and testify that the Father has sent his Son to be the Saviour of the world. (1 John 4:7-14)

...REFLECTION...

We have lived in various different places and each time the soil has been different.

Sometimes it's been like clay, claggy, needing additives and requiring much work. Other times it may have been a rich fine soil in which plants would flourish more easily.

This is pretty true of us. At times our hearts can be hard and clogged up with stuff, maybe through the conditioning of circumstances or upbringing. Life influences us. We need additives too, 'soil enhancers' to loosen up our spirit to enable fruitfulness to develop within us. This is the sanctifying work of the Holy Spirit within us. This is the fruit of the Spirit growing and maturing into fullness and into favour in our lives, where we are able to more fully demonstrate the wonder working power of God.

The parable of the sower is presented to us in all of the 'synoptic gospels', so it's an important message for us to hear regarding planting and harvesting.

Here are the different types of soil in the passage:

1. The hard ground by the wayside; where seed cannot grow at all.
2. The stony ground, where seeds germinate but fail to take root as there is no depth of soil. The plant withers and dies.

3. The thorny ground; where the plant begins to grow well, but is soon choked by the thorns that surround them.
4. The good ground; the good stuff, where the seed grows until it produces much fruit.

This may be primarily a picture of salvation and of hearts ready to receive the gospel. But it also shows us where we need to be in our spiritual walk, where we need a little spiritual fertiliser added into our hardened hearts.

Our 'Kings' that we looked at are perfect (and very imperfect) examples of how we often are before God, and I think that if we are honest, we can probably see ourselves in one or another of the attitudes that they displayed.

Best to have a regular review and aim for the good ground where the blessing grows. Thirty fold, sixty fold and a hundred fold are all offered, as we sow into the word of God, live obediently and walk by faith. We reap what we sow, so we must sow well.

SECTION 2

TALKING OF TESTIFYING...

CONTENTS

Chapter 7.

FAITH AND FAITHFULNESS –

In The Testimony

They overcame him by the blood of the lamb and
by the word of their testimony…
Rev 12:11 (NKJV)

Today it was a 'Testimony Sunday' at our church. People gave testimony of how God had revealed himself in a new way over the past year. From miracles of healing to more courage to speak of faith to an unbeliever, of those in need asking for prayer, recognising that there is a God who is the only one who can answer that need. Also of walking through the dark valley of sudden bereavement with the help of the loving and almighty God.

We finished section one, with the apostle John expressing the importance of being able to testify of what he has seen and heard, in the Father sending the Son to be the saviour of the world.

In this section we are going to major on the testimony of faith in the goodness of God. It was apt that on this day the regular 'preach' was replaced by the testimonies that summed up the year for many, coming at the close of this year and with anticipation of the New Year ahead in the service of our Lord.

The root of the word for testimony in Latin interprets as 'covenant'. The Bible is a book made up of the Old Covenant and the New Covenant, as we know, or better known as the Old and New Testament. This implies that the Bible reveals God's testimony to mankind of his character and his nature.

The root for testimony in Hebrew actually interprets 'to do it again' - or 'to repeat'. [7]

We have looked at successive covenants in the Old Testament, all leading to the fulfilment of the New Covenant. There are repeated prophecies and repeated testimonies throughout Scripture to encourage us, to keep us on track, to build our trust and our faith in this God who we want to know in a richer and deeper way.

Adding On The V.A.T....

'V.A.T.' or value added tax, was introduced in 1973. It is of course a tax that is placed upon the value of a product usually hidden within the overall price. We are now going to be talking V.A.T. Before you think that I have lost the plot, we are not referring to the value added tax, which we don't like at all, but to the 'value added testimony', which we do like, very much.

Testimony has been added to, or included in the truth of scripture from the beginning of Genesis to the end of Revelation, and then onward in and through our own lives, (or it should be!).

In Genesis chapter 1 when God was creating, after everything he created he then stood back, took a look and declared that, 'It was good!'. That was the Father, Son and Spirit testifying to one another and to the world.

The final verses of Revelation read; 'He who testifies to these things says, "Yes I am coming soon." Amen. Come, Lord Jesus. The grace of the Lord Jesus be with God's people. Amen' (Rev 22:20-21).

That's us, friends, the redeemed, testifying to one another, and to the world.

John the Baptist spent his ministry life testifying of the 'greater one who was coming'. When John baptises Jesus in Matt 3, the Father testifies of Jesus: "this is my Son, whom I love; with him I am well pleased." Jesus testifies to John about the Father in Luke 7, when in a moment of uncertainty, John asks if Jesus is truly the one, or is there another yet to come? Jesus replies, "the blind see, the lame walk, lepers are cured, the deaf hear, the dead are raised, and the good news is preached to the poor!" (v.22, *Para*). That is the gospel, found in the person of the Messiah.

If you have moments of uncertainty you are not alone. John lost his head, literally. What was that about? It affected Jesus for sure. He took himself off to a lonely place by himself where he could reassess and re-engage his mission. He went on immediately healing all who came to him. He didn't give up, but instead carried on his ministry of bringing in the Kingdom of God in all its fullness wherever he could, because that is what defeats the enemy, whose mission is to destroy the testimony of the people of God. The message here is to keep going, even in the toughest times that are so hard to understand.

Remember how much those who were healed by Jesus wanted or needed to give testimony to their healing, even when they were told not to. They just couldn't help but declare of God's goodness. In fact Jesus himself said that even the stones would cry out of the goodness of God if people kept silent.

"If they kept quiet, the stones along the road would burst into cheers!" (Luke 19:40, NLT).

Remember how after Mary recognises the risen Jesus she rushes to tell the other disciples. How the men travelling to Emmaus after realising that Jesus had had been with them, raced back to Jerusalem to tell the others. They didn't wait until morning. They were probably pretty tired, it's a seven miles hike back but good news is good news and sometimes it just can't wait!

David kicks off Psalm 9 by saying: 'I will give thanks to you, Lord, with all my heart; I will tell of all your wonderful deeds.'

Psalm 96:3 says, 'Declare his glory among all nations, his marvellous deeds among all peoples.' The New Living Translation has, 'Publish his glorious deeds among the nations. Tell everyone about the amazing things he does.' This Psalm is attributed to Moses. Here are 2 giants of faith and testimony, forerunners of the Messiah.

Testimony is absolutely value added truth as another way of putting it. It gladdens the heart, enriches the spirit, opens the mind and brings a big smile to the face. It helps to bring light into the darkness.

Isn't the news quite depressing? Often! Occasionally the newsreader will have a really 'nice' story to finish a programme. Do you see the smile on the face, the tear in the eye? Do you feel that smile and that tear yourself? I do. I love to hear a positive, heart -warming testimony. We need to hear more of them I believe.

There is nothing like a testimony to confirm a word from God and to seal a truth into our hearts, bringing a promise or a revelation alive. To both the believer and the unbeliever alike. It may turn an unbeliever into a believer.

On a car journey recently together with my wife and daughter, I start eating a madeleine, that's a little shell shaped French sponge cake if you need to know. I was a back seat passenger. When the girls realised I was swiftly told - 'but you had yours earlier'. There were three left! Oops. A couple of hours had passed since that cake was eaten and there appeared to be little interest from the front seats regarding eating those cakes, especially as my daughter who was driving was consuming an iced bun. It was my wife who clearly had foreknowledge of how many 'madeleines' were still in the bag. That's troubling in itself!

I stopped eating immediately and offered the remaining half along with the unopened one in the packet. 'No, we don't want one' was the response, so I finish my cake and then suddenly a voice says, ok, we will have it now! How can a man understand the mind of a woman?

In order to play fair and even the playing field, I have to admit that it is sometimes difficult for a man to hear a request from a woman and remember to do it. When she asks; 'have you done what I asked?' you are racking the little grey cells to remember what it was she wanted so that you don't look inept. If you can *just* remember, you can quickly do it and she won't know any different! Worse still when you ask if she would like you to do something in particular and she replies, 'I asked you that earlier'. That leads to the terrible 'you never listen to me' line and the humble reply. 'Sorry I honestly don't remember you asking me that'. I think that a lot of girlfriends and wives reading this might be nodding just now. Aren't you...?

You see, our antenna is not finely tuned to accurately hear what is being said through all the white noise, or so it would appear!

At times we seem to be like a different species of being. The depths of the mind and understanding of the thinking process is somewhat unfathomable.

It's the same with nations. We pulled our caravan into a site near La Rochelle. Great, we thought, not many here, in for a quiet weekend. By mid afternoon it seemed that half of France (and the noisy half) had descended upon the campsite. Not so great. Making enquiries we discovered that there was a big boules competition that weekend!

Boules is everywhere in France. People just pull up seemingly anywhere, and out come the silver balls, the tape measure and the notepad. It's serious business. Another campsite in the Ardeche, we would drive off for the day, sightseeing, leaving the boules players hard at it to find them still playing when we returned. Why come on holiday we wondered, to this lovely spot just to throw balls around all day. It's all boules and moules it seems. Two hours off for lunch and at 7pm it's time for the French to hit the pavement café for a bowl of *moules et frites*, and a bottle of red, lazing in the evening sun. (Perhaps rather stereotyped!)

Over in the UK, it's work all day, no time for little pleasures. Grab a sandwich or a bag of good ol' fish and chips on the go, whilst dodging the rain showers....

As I pushed my trolley around the supermarché a little French lady peered in. She looked up at me inquisitively. 'C'est Chinois!' I offered. I had found ingredients to make a Chinese Stir Fry. She looked doubtful. 'And you eat this food...?'

Behind our house was communal land where there was a Grande fête each summer. The fireworks over the river were grand, but not so sure about the games.

They had marked out an area with squares and we sat in the garden wondering what this could be. We suggested a sack race perhaps, or leap frog, perhaps a French hopscotch? Once the fête was open I walked across intrigued. By now there was a cow in this enclosure. Bizarre! It was 'a lotto'. The winner is the one who guesses 'which square the cow does a poo in'. Oh how marvellous. I'm quite sure the French have their misgivings about us too. They're just across the water but seem a world away. We look a lot alike, but we each love to do things that the other doesn't even consider. How about further afield? Another continent? Take moss. We hate the stuff, dig it up and eradicate it wherever we find it. The Japanese however, apparently revere their moss and cultivate it. We are indeed, all very different!

In the spiritual sense, being born again of what the Bible calls, incorruptible seed, does in reality lead us to become a different species of being. Our DNA is now in Christ; we are transformed into the image of God and made co-heirs with Christ according to the promise. We look the same as everyone else but in our spirit we have been eternally renewed. Whilst we still live in the flesh in a corruptible body, our soul, made up of our mind, our will and emotions, are still programmed to follow the flesh as opposed to the spirit man which desires only to follow the path of redemptive grace, the way of salvation and seeking after the will and purpose of God in our lives. Here lies the conundrum, the tension of life in the spirit with the fuel of faith of the unseen, and the life of the flesh, fuelled by the knowledge of what can be seen and measured.

What did Paul say in Romans 7? In his inner being he can delight in God's law, but he sees another law at work waging war against this desire and making him feel like a prisoner of sin at work within him. 'Wretched man that I am! Who will deliver me from this body of death? Thanks be to God through Jesus Christ our Lord.' (Rom 7:24-25a, ESV). He goes on to say that there is now no condemnation for those who are in Christ Jesus in chapter 8 v1. This whole section of Romans needs to be read in its entirety to gain the fullness of the gospel message of faith within it.

'So then faith comes by hearing, and hearing by the word of God' (Rom 10:17, NKJV). Or: '...the Good News about Christ' (NLT).

To grow faith, to hear God more clearly and fully, we must 'water with the word.'

Coming to faith is a one-time experience through the revelation of sins forgiven, of life eternal and being made in the image of God.

Living and speaking faith is how the Kingdom operates.

Faithfulness is an on going heart purpose to follow the master, to be just like him in all that we are and all that we do and all that it costs.

The 'Awe-Full' Decision...

During the period following the Welsh Revival many preachers went out to share the gospel in other lands. One such missionary went to the Assam region in North East India. He preached to a tribe of Head Hunters, but only one man would listen and come to faith in God, leaving his ancestral gods behind. The chief was furious at this conversion and told him to renounce his faith or die. The young man said: 'I have decided to follow Jesus, there's no turning back.' At this the young man's children were shot with arrows. 'Renounce or your wife will die too.' 'Though no one joins me, still I will follow, no turning back' was the response. His wife was killed too, and unrepentant the young man declared once more his decision: 'the cross before me, the world behind me, no turning back,' and also lost his life.

The missionary had left, what good can come from such an awful scenario as this. What a failure. Where was God?

That same village was visited some years later by the missionary; who was to find that there was now a large established church there and the tribe worshipping God. Revival had broken out.

After the young convert had died the chief began to wonder. Who was this man Jesus from so far away and so long ago, that he could influence this family to the extent that they were willing to die for belief in his salvation? Only revelation by the Holy Spirit can change a man and this man was changed. The testimony of the young man was so powerful that the chief accepted Christ as did the whole tribe, and faith began there in that region of Assam.

It is where the song was born: 'I have decided to follow Jesus, no turning back, no turning back.' The martyrs last words were put to a traditional Assam tune by Indian evangelist Sadhu Singh that has been sung throughout the generations.

> Will you decide now to follow Jesus?
> Will you decide now to follow Jesus?
> Will you decide now to follow Jesus?
> No turning back, no turning back.[8]

Surely this must be the ultimate testimony of absolute faith and faithfulness.

Unseen by the eye of the flesh but seen only through the eye of the spirit, the perspective of heaven is revealed in eternity.

Chapter 8.

JUDGEMENT AND JUSTICE –
Set Free!

I think we think that God thinks like we think...

Can we get mad at God? Do we get mad with God? Fortunately we have plenty of examples of some of the greatest prophets, Kings and servants in scripture who did just that. Remember how David had to tough it out for so long with many cries of 'How long oh Lord before you answer me?' Remember his frustration with the Uzzah incident that we talked about earlier. How he walked away thinking something like; 'I can't do this anymore'. What about Elijah in 1 Kings 19? After such amazing success over the prophets of Baal he took to running with the Jezebel threat, no doubt burnt out and exhausted, spiritually and physically. We'll look more at that in the next chapter.

David saw the connection between judgement and justice: 'Arise, Lord, in your anger; rise up against the rage of my enemies. Awake my God; decree justice.' (Ps 7:6). Then in v.8, 'Let the Lord judge the people's. Vindicate me Lord, according to my integrity, O most high.'

This is the expected and experienced world - view that we have. Where wrong is done there must be justice sought, and judgement is the method that has to be made against the offender - Sounds reasonable doesn't it?

Jen Wilkin brings some context into the three characteristics of God, which came out of the Ten Commandments in Ex 34.

'The relationship of justice, mercy and grace.'

Justice. Is getting what we deserve.
Mercy. Is not getting what we deserve.
Grace. Is getting what we do not deserve.

She quotes later from 1 John 1:9: 'If we confess our sins, he is faithful and just to forgive us our sins and to cleanse us from all unrighteousness.'

She goes on to explain how she was confounded by the word 'just'. 'Shouldn't it say "faithful and merciful" not "faithful and just"?'

Surely it's not 'just' to forgive us. Surely, given who we are and what we are like it has to be mercy? Explaining further, Jen Wilkin gives us a testimony of an incident where she ran a red light. A ticket was issued with photo evidence and a fine to clear her good name. However it was actually her husband's good name that needed to be restored as she was driving his car at the time. He paid the ticket for her. As far as the state of Texas was concerned, justice was done. He received what she deserved; the ticket was taken care of, but by another. [9]

I am reminded of a line in the movie, *National Treasure*. Following the theft of the American Declaration of independence (all for a good reason if you've seen the film), Nicholas Cage is told, 'someone's gotta go to prison'. A penalty must be paid.

The judgement of us all came upon Jesus at the cross. He paid the cost, and justice was made on our behalf. Mercy was the result. Just as we read, 'anyone who was hung on a tree was cursed' - he bore our curse and pronounced us justified.

Here's my driving testimony, the result being strikingly similar to that of Jen Wilkin.

I was around 18. I hadn't long passed my driving test. I lived on the South coast in Eastbourne. Without too much expectation I asked my Dad if I could borrow his car to drive to Oban in Scotland for two weeks with my friend Andy Lancaster. To my amazement he agreed, which meant that he was walking to work while I went off for a jolly in his nice Peugeot 304. Crazy perhaps.

All went well as we arrived in Scotland. Nice hot day, shirts off, windows open. Music playing. Hey, look at us. 'Lads out on the town'. Then came the Scottish rain. We drove into a car park. Everything was misted up. It was pouring. I was pretty sure there was a space behind me. I reversed into it. There wasn't.

I deemed it too wet to get out of the car to check and *crunch* came the result.

It was a good one. Minimal damage to the Peugeot. A very solid car, but a lovely dent right in the middle of the grill of the other guy! It was a Ford Consul or Granada, very smart, with a large badge in the centre of the grill, which I took out neatly with the addition of a big dent.

The choice was to run, after all, no one has seen it except us, and of course God. We were both 'good Christian boys' and that thought was only fleeting if at all. We went inside the restaurant holding up the badge like a prize, and asked for the owner of the vehicle. I confessed humbly, was as penitent as possible and I gave him my insurance details. Well, to be precise, my father's insurance details.

He was now my father and not so much my dad, I thought. I phoned him to give him the bad news, stressing that he probably only required a paint job - and stressing over what his reaction might be...

His response was incredible and I have never forgotten it. His first words were, 'are you alright son?' His interest was only for our wellbeing and not for himself. 'Forget all about it now and enjoy your time, stay safe.' We did. I gave him the details of the insurance of the other driver and never thought about it, never dealt with it, never paid toward it: Justice was met by my father taking the judgement, and I received the mercy. Grace unmerited was mine. Marvellous eh?

God doesn't think in the way that we think. I could have run that day and not owned up to my failure. Then I would have missed out on the rescue. I wouldn't have had that experience of receiving favour from my Dad. Like the prodigal son, as soon as he appeared on the Father's horizon, the Father is the one who took to running. Towards the one who had slipped up, to welcome him home. To say, 'Are you alright son?'

The thing is, God is kind, he is patient and he is long suffering. The fruits of the Spirit are the fruit of God's character.

Maybe you have slipped up, maybe you think that you're too far gone for God to look upon you, and to receive you with the same mercy as he extends to others.

A parable Jesus told in Matt 20 was of workers that worked hard for the vineyard owner all day for an agreed price. Successive employees were set to work at various times through the day and at the end the landowner paid them all the same amount. Of course the first workers were furious that some had done so little but received so much. They thought it unjust, but of course translated into God's kingdom this displays his absolute justice and mercy to us who are deserving of none.

It's just not done in our world. We can get pretty upset pretty easily. How do we feel when the unpleasant neighbour seems to prosper? How did *we* feel when our not so pleasant neighbour was taken away after a police raid, and a corporate sigh of relief went up from the street, only for him to return just a few days later singing louder than ever; 'they can't get nothing on me!'

How about when that person that we struggle with is prospering and making sure you know about it. Everything is going just perfect for them, and they keep causing trouble. Do we secretly hope that they might just trip up along the way. If something goes awry then we can feel better about ourselves. Aha, justice at last - but it doesn't happen and we're still struggling and still mad at God.

Yes, his justice seems often 'topsy turvy', upside down, back to front and inside out. If only God would take them down a peg or two...

This was definitely how one of the prophets felt. This was a story as much about the prophet himself, as of the events proclaimed by the prophet. His name was of course Jonah. We know the story. Called to preach repentance to the city of Nineveh, he took to running as far as could possibly get in the opposite direction. He couldn't stand the Assyrians. They were opposed to God. They were idolaters. They hated what Jonah stood for. They were ruthless people. He despised them and so should have God.

Running the other way he figured, he was really doing God a favour. Had God said 'go preach to them destruction and that's what I'm going to give them whether they repent or not', he would have been the man for the job. First on the scene. That was his view on judgement and justice. No mercy. He defends his viewpoint by thinking that he is just jealous for God's good name, but it's not how the Kingdom of God works.

Of course he has to be obedient to the second call, the nation repents and God extends mercy to the people. God is so much kinder than Jonah, he even thinks about the animals and not just the people. Jonah sees rebellion but God sees restoration. Jonah's reaction?

That's it. I knew it. That's just typical of you God. Kind and compassionate and forgiving. I want to wipe them out!

So how does that leave Jonah? Unhappy, messed up, depressed and wanting to die. Not ideal to be honest.

Let's not be taking to judgemental attitudes. If we want to be forgiven by our Father in heaven we have to forgive. If we say that we are 'believing in faith' for supernatural answers to prayer, but we are unforgiving ourselves, that faith won't work. It's fundamental in God's kingdom. Unforgiveness grows into a root of bitterness.

Jesus gives us a parable in Matt 18:21-35 where a Master forgave a servant a huge debt that was clearly un-payable. He cancelled the debt, but the forgiven servant went to another servant who owed him a very small amount and had him thrown in prison for not being able to pay him back. The result was that the Master after hearing of this then put the unforgiving servant in prison himself for showing no mercy.

Faith only works within the framework of love. Outside of love our freedom is lost. A beautiful bouquet of flowers can only stay that way for a short time because they have been cut from the root. The universe, including you and I have been created that way, by faith, but grounded in love. Take away the love - and lose the faith that brings the freedom, the healing, the prosperity of the gospel and the peace of mind in God that passes all understanding. These things just can't work or survive outside of the framework of love. Within the ark there was safety, outside of the ark there was a whole sea of trouble!

Jesus said: 'I tell you, you can pray for anything, and if you believe that you've received it, it will be yours. *But* when you are praying, first forgive anyone you are holding a grudge against, so that your Father in heaven will forgive your sins too' (Mark 11:24-25, NLT). (Italics added.)

Mercy trumps justice. 'Speak and act as those who are going to be judged by the law that gives freedom, because judgement without mercy will be shown to anyone who has not been merciful. Mercy triumphs over judgement!' (James 2:12-13). We often look at people and make our own decisions on their character, even if we have no background knowledge. We go by appearance, but God doesn't go by appearances. He looks at the heart. It's a lesson we all need to revise, regularly. Well I do anyway! 'Who is a God like you, pardoning iniquity?' (Micah 7:18a, ESV).

Another renowned character, in a sense rather like Jonah, had at one time an incomplete understanding of the heart of God, was Martin Luther in the 16th century - but with the benefit of grace found in the New Covenant.

The great reformer Martin Luther admitted his head knowledge of the righteousness of a God who hates sin. This caused him not to love but even to 'hate such a God who punishes sinners'. He says 'I was angry with God'. This only produced a transfer of affection on to Mary and other saints. But through the revelation of the Holy Spirit, he later declared that, 'It is not enough to know God as creator and judge. He has to be known also as a loving Father. Through the Son the Father can be seen, it brings assurance and joy and wins our hearts to him, for "we may look into his Fatherly heart and sense how boundlessly he loves us. That would warm our hearts, setting them aglow with thankfulness."' [10]

It is therefore in the true revelation of God that we find the true faith that sets us free.

Chapter 9.

REST AND RESTORATION –

Renewed

And this is what he has promised us -
Eternal Life. 1 John 2:25

He was ready to pack it in. That's it, he said in verse 4 of 1 Kings 19. 'I have had enough Lord, take my life; I am no better than my ancestors.' He then lay down for a much needed sleep and an angel came and cooked him breakfast, then another doze, and then; *'dinner's ready'*!

Ever felt like this? Most of us can probably identify with this darkness of spirit that can lead us into depression. A downward cycle of despair can be so destructive and so hard to climb out from. It happens, and we need a rescuer to lift us back up again.

Elijah said, 'It's only me that's left'. Well, that's an exaggeration. Actually it's seriously understating the truth but it's so easy to get like that. Nobody really bothers with me, no one actually cares, I'm nothing, when in reality a lot of people do care and God most certainly does. He comes not in the big rushing wind, not in the earthquake, not in the fire, the big things that perhaps we are hoping for, but he just comes quietly. If we look and listen, and he says, 'What are you doing in this place?' v.13, it is time to get back on track, start trusting again. No judgement, just re-visioning.

Elijah had just come from massive success in overthrowing the enemies of God and demonstrating the One All Powerful God to the nation, to find that the king and the queen were not in the least persuaded or convicted of their sin. Only outraged even further with the threat of impending death for Elijah. He went from the highest to the lowest in a moment. It's a natural human response when suddenly we are in distress and it requires divine intervention, which was the case here for Elijah. He was strengthened by an angel of the Lord: he was fed, he was encouraged and he rested until he was ready for a forty day journey, where he met God in the gentlest way. The whisper of God is not loud, he's not shouting at us and he needs us to 'Be still and know that I am God' (Ps 46:10a).

It's good to talk, it's fine to ask someone for help, it's great to be prayed for; but even better is to wait before God and listen for his voice. In a multimedia age that takes some determination.

Having a difficult time walking with God? Jeremiah was definitely having a bad day in his book of Lamentations. He talks about his distress - he talks about his torment, of how the sin of the people has brought the anger of God. He identifies with the people, he feels afflicted, in darkness, prayers are hitting the ceiling, everyone dislikes him anyway and he's lost his prospects and his peace. But suddenly as he considers how downcast he has become, he reaches out for the promise of God. 'Yet this I call to mind and therefore I have hope: Because of the Lord's great love we are not consumed, for his compassions never fail. They are new every morning; great is your faithfulness. I say to myself, "The Lord is my portion, therefore I will wait for him." The Lord is good to those whose hope is in him, to the one who seeks him; it is good to wait quietly for the salvation of the Lord' (Lam 3:21-26).

This is both a well known and a beautiful scripture describing how God is always faithful, his mercies don't grow old and wear out, they are renewed daily. Wait on God and embrace his love. His renewal will be along any moment.

David has a similar attitude in Ps 27. He starts by putting his confidence in the Lord. 'The Lord is my light and salvation - whom shall I fear? The Lord is the stronghold of my life - of whom shall I be afraid?' He goes on to mention his considerable problems and all that is attacking him, but simply rolls it all over on to God in v4. 'One thing I ask of the Lord, this is what I seek: that I may dwell in the house of the Lord all the days of my life, to gaze upon the beauty of the Lord and to seek him in his temple.' He continues in the same vein, that he will seek God regardless of the trouble that comes and closes out the chapter by saying, 'I remain confident of this: I will see the goodness of the Lord in the land of the living. Wait for the Lord; be strong and take heart and wait for the Lord.' v 13-14. One translation emphasises further, 'take courage and *wait I say*, wait for the Lord.' I love that emphasis. (Italics added.)

When I think of Jesus in the wilderness, Satan came at his most vulnerable and attacked him at his weakest. Like Elijah, it was forty days and nights. Hungry, tired and alone, he was tempted in three ways that John explains in 1 John 2:16.

1. The lust of the flesh.
2. The lust of the eye.
3. The pride of life.

In essence Satan said, I'll give you exactly what you need right now. Instant gratification.

Just let go...

1. Let me indulge you now. It's good to taste.
2. I can give you everything that you can see or desire.
3. Make a big statement. Show them who you really are.

He was pulling the same stunt on Jesus as he did with Adam and Eve in Gen 3.

But Jesus wasn't buying. He wasn't taking the bait. God was there. He wasn't alone.

Where mankind had dropped the baton and fallen, Jesus took hold of the baton and stood, in the authority of the Holy Spirit, overcoming the enemy, and in that moment the reversal of the work of Satan and establishing of the Kingdom was made possible.

These are the three areas that include all the sin that we could commit, especially if we love the world more than the Father, as John quotes in 1 John 2:15. They sum up what Satan himself had coveted, and Jesus so beautifully quotes from Deuteronomy the truth of scripture, of seeking God first, the truth that is in the word and in the worship.

1. Man does not live on bread alone.
2. Worship the Lord your God and serve him only.
3. Do not put the Lord your God to the test.

Rebuking Satan with scripture is vital, and revisiting and renewing faith with scripture is equally vital. Zech 3:1-2 has this to encourage us: 'Then he showed me Joshua (*a variant of Jeshua*) the high priest standing before the angel of the Lord, and Satan standing at his right side to accuse him. The Lord said to Satan, "The Lord rebuke you, Satan! The Lord who has chosen Jerusalem, rebuke you! Is not this man a burning stick snatched from the fire?"' (Italics added.)

Satan is always the accuser and abuser, but God is always the redemptive restorer. In verse 4 we read: 'the angel said to those who were standing before him, "Take off his filthy clothes." Then he said to Joshua, "see, I have taken away your sin, and I will put fine garments on you."'

We have been snatched as it were from the fire of judgement, through Jesus overcoming Satan in his time of trial and temptation, and in the victory of a sinless death upon the cross. We can turn and rebuke Satan with the same faith as Jesus, purely because of Jesus. Clothed in his purity.

Have I always done this myself? Sadly no, I really haven't, not nearly enough. But God is a God of restoration, as we reside in him, and rest in his presence, he draws close to us as we draw near to him.

Satan's sole plan is to circumvent God's purposes for our lives. It was just the same as he intended to do with Jesus, in Luke 4. To depend on or to worship anything other than God takes us off the path that we should be walking on. Hence the sharp rebuke of The Lord to Satan through the power of the Spirit.

To get us into a position of guilt before God brings unease into our lives, it diminishes our sense of relationship and reduces our level of faith. It disturbs our ability to be able to rest in God the Father. It causes us to strive to please God and God doesn't want us to strive, that's Satan's motive to get us offside with the Father.

We often strive to display more of the fruit of the Spirit in our lives, but the fruit of the Spirit comprises the character of God, they are in fact the nature of God.

'But the fruit of Spirit is love, joy, peace, patience, kindness, goodness, faithfulness, gentleness, self control; against such things there is no law' (Gal 5:22-23, ESV). In other words, nothing stands against us from knowing the Christ like character of God. The Message Bible reads, 'Legalism is helpless in bringing this about; it only gets in the way.' So don't press, don't struggle and don't strive. Just invest in God and in the word, rest in the Father's embrace.

We were moving back to the UK from France. It was 2016 and we had wondered why we had been waiting a while for a buyer. It so happened that the day we sold, and euros went into our account, was the day of the 'Brexit' vote result. The exchange rate had favoured us transferring sterling to euros whilst we were living in France but not so good transferring it the other way, especially when you want to buy a property back in the

UK. Of course the 'out vote' meant a sharp drop in the value of the Pound, which boosted our sale money by a fairly significant amount overnight. This made such a difference to our ability to re-establish the right home in the right place and allowed the Lord to close and open doors for us to locate our new home. It was unplanned but it happened that we came across a 3 storey versatile property with a top floor that we could make into an apartment for our daughter who was also in need of a new home.

In November of 2016, three weeks before our completion date, I travelled by train from Shrewsbury to Eastbourne, and suddenly while visiting friends for an evening meal I had a brain seizure, as I have mentioned earlier in the book. It so happened that my friend Mike, whom I was with, had been a paramedic and he knew exactly what to do. I awoke in the ambulance with paramedics trying to restore my vital signs.

I know that I was in and out of consciousness and that they were working on me in the hospital. Mike came down and graciously stayed with me all night while his wife Carla phoned my wife Carole, and daughter Becci; who suddenly found themselves driving through the night, at this point unsure of the severity of the situation.

Following a CT scan I was given an MRI scan where a brain tumour was discovered.

I think that night Mike probably saved my life acting so quickly and with his knowledge. I was in the right place if this was going to happen. I could have been in the car that I had borrowed, and was driving just a few minutes earlier. I could have been in the guest flat at my mother's home where no one would know anything had happened, or on the earlier train journey through

London. But I wasn't. I was in safe hands. 'The Father's hands.'

My cousin David, who was a GP, came down from the Wirral to support me, and people began to pray around the country and further afield in other countries.

I stayed in a ward for 4 days and during that time the oncologist came to see me with the initial MRI result. 'It's not very good news I'm afraid' she said. It looks like you could have a grade 3 or 4 tumour. I found our later that there are four grades, 1-4 and while the lower two are usually benign, the higher two are malignant. She said, rather matter of fact that it was likely that I would only live for 15 months.

Strangely I felt no fear. Maybe I was not quite in full knowledge of the severity of the situation, or *maybe* I was able to draw upon the testimony of God in my life. There had been miraculous times of healing and deliverance to take faith from, the testimony of scripture and the perfect love of God that casts out all fear, and the testimony of his immediate peace that was upon me.

I shared the report with David but not with other family at this point, until we could get an appointment to see the specialist at Stoke Hospital, which has an excellent reputation. - Although the car parking facility and food was not so much. A yellow substance masquerading as custard was most intriguing - and almost edible!

We were advised not to try moving house, especially one with 3 floors, but we felt it was right to go ahead and moved in on the 2nd December. I prayed for strength and am convinced that God gave me the strength for that day. Although being very weak, I lifted a front door right off its hinges with such strength it hit the ceiling! (In order to get a large tub chair out of my daughters flat!)

We also had help in moving things into our new home from friends at Church, which was of course invaluable.

We didn't know that I would not be driving again for several years, my wife would have to pick up the driving again after a long absence, but as it turns out, our house is opposite the bus stop. The bus takes us into Shrewsbury, which is ten miles away and goes right by the hospital, which became our second home with several months of continued treatment of radiotherapy and chemotherapy.

It became clear how important it was that we had chosen to live in a place that was so accessible to medical facilities, and that our daughter was on hand to help with daily needs. This is how the Lord leads and provides for us along the way.

The first thing was an operation at Stoke, to remove what could be safely removed before local treatment began. The surgeon was more upbeat about the prognosis, but the Shrewsbury team is a little more pragmatic and follows the statistics. They initially suggested that I would have 6 months to live without treatment and 18 months with it. There were many support groups that were available but we chose not to get involved with anything that could bring negative thoughts into our minds, but to focus particularly on the Psalms, especially with Ian White's musical renditions.

Songs From Heaven...

In the July of 2016 Carole had bought me a birthday gift, a watercolour painting of a treble clef with the words, 'There's a song being sung over you' from Zephaniah

3:17. This was a few months before the seizure. Following the seizure and around the time of the operation in January 2017 Carole's sister sent a message. Unaware of the picture with its text she felt the Lord prompting her to send me the same scripture, 'He will rejoice over you with singing.' This was encouraging and was to become more so.

In May 2017 at a specific prayer meeting for my health through the treatment, and ultimate healing, Anna had a word from God for me. She didn't give it to me during the meeting, as she really wasn't sure about it. She gave it to me later. You know what it was now don't you? 'Yes it really is right' I replied. I knew that God was looking out for my wellbeing and that I was in his thoughts and on his heart. As I write these very words a song has just come on UCB radio. 'Before I spoke a word you are singing over me.' God is in the testimony!

A friend from Eastbourne phoned me in Feb 2017. While praying for you and reading Psalm 91, I felt that the Lord wants to tell you, 'He will call on me, and I will answer him; I will be with him in trouble, I will deliver him and honour him. With long life I will satisfy him and show him my salvation' (Ps 91:15-16).

Following my intense periods of treatment, the MRI scan was unclear of any improvement. This I was told was normal because of how the radiotherapy affects the imaging. A further scan which would be more telling, and then for the results. An anxious moment as we swung out of the house for the hospital and the daily reading verse had popped up on the mobile. 'With long life I will satisfy him and show him my salvation.' Wow. Lord, you have my full attention. 'How good it is to be loved by you.'

Let me encourage you to testify of the goodness of God. As I write this testimony my faith is being built up. 'We overcome the enemy of our faith by the blood of the lamb and the word of our testimony' (Rev 12:11, *Para*).

I had been put on a high dose of steroids after the seizure and Stoke were keen to reduce the dose as soon as possible. I lay awake at night a lot and it was during this time that I sensed a newness and nearness of God that I had not experienced before. It proved to be a pivotal moment in this journey.

The sense of His presence was tangible, and where most people would hate to lay there awake and unable to sleep, I found myself enjoying being with the Father.

I was sleeping mostly at this time in the spare room so as not to disturb my wife, and Mr Bobbins the cat, often cuddled up and slept next to me. I would probably throw him off me now, but at that time I really didn't mind. He was almost a comfort to me, which is hard to admit! Animals do have a sense of when people are unwell.

I felt that God was showing me things and teaching me things that I hadn't truly grasped deeply within my spirit previously.

In the nearness of God's presence my thoughts were racing. I began to think of the times when I hadn't listened to God, that I'd gone my way, ignored him, sinned against him and generally failed him. I went through my 'naughty list' and waited for chastisement. There was silence in heaven and suddenly I realised that there was no 'naughty list'. Not any longer. Jesus had bought and paid for the list, past, present and future and erased it at the cross. What I knew in my mind came alive in my spirit in the presence of *the* Holy Spirit, and all that

I sensed was the extreme compassion of the Father. I felt the compassion of Jesus. The Scripture tells us often that when he was healing the sick, Jesus first had compassion on the person. This compassion goes far beyond our human compassion. It is divine in its nature. In the Greek language the word compassion is translated from the strongest form of its expression.

There can be a real sense of shame that comes over us in suddenly being the recipient of a serious illness. Thoughts can easily come into the mind to make us believe that perhaps somehow we have been at fault, when in fact there are many reasons why disease is around us and often times within us. Sometimes they might be spiritual, often times just the natural cause of a fallen world. Cancer can be seen as from Hell itself. It destroys the body and the mind, and if it were at all possible, the spirit of a man, or a woman. It is certainly a weapon of Satan in this world today to undermine all that the Father has done for us in the restoration of the physical and spiritual realm.

As I said before, these were my initial thoughts as I entered God's presence, until he so quickly and lovingly showed me that there was no shame on my part.

You may be sensing that somehow you are a 'second class' believer if you are struggling, or have been struggling with illness for some time. You wonder what others might think. You don't want to be constantly asking, or going out for prayer in church. It feels as though your level of faith is at stake here.

Sometimes there are issues, maybe generational issues that need breaking off, or un-forgiveness, inner turmoil or lifestyles that can contribute to being unwell, but these are all areas that one can seek counselling for, and are beneficial. However, the majority of people that Jesus healed were simply sick because there was sickness in the world!

What did Paul say to Timothy? 'Don't let anyone look down on you because you are young, but set an example for the believers in speech, in life, in love, in faith and in purity' (1 Tim 4:12). The same applies I believe. Don't feel that anyone is looking down on you or that somehow you are failing. You are not. 'You are precious in his sight.'

We were in a church (which will remain nameless) and invited by some of the leaders to go for counselling. We had concerns but thought that perhaps it was common practice to offer support and encouragement. Our concerns however, were not unfounded. We were questioned instead over the condition of our marriage, due to our children who were not at that time following the Lord in the way that their children were! Needless to say we left that session in tears, now in *need* of help and actual counselling from a brother in the Lord.

This left us with a distrust of leaders for quite some time, as if they were 'first class' believers and we certainly weren't. This should not be, my friends in the family of God. We are all bought and made one by the same Holy Spirit, and if you ever feel that maybe it's your fault that you have certain issues that haven't yet been resolved, then stop it now please! Satan is *the* accuser of the brethren, not God, nor should it be anyone else.

This is true for sickness, family problems, life's difficulties, financial issues and anything else that the enemy wants to throw in our direction in order to destroy our faith in an Almighty God whose love and compassion is immeasurable.

The Shame And Glory Of The Cross...

God had to operate at this divine level of love and compassion to have ever considered us to the degree that he would send his only Son as the propitiation for our sins. He has assumed our guilt and shame, become our substitute and expiated that guilt in order to render us blameless and holy in his sight. There really is no better news. So, rest in his love. You have been restored, renewed.

Chapter 10.

ATONEMENT AND ADVOCACY –
The Just Judge

Mind the gap...

I sat in the courtroom facing my accusers. The presiding magistrate looked over at me. 'I'm giving you three months' he said. Wow, that's great I thought. Thank you!

You see it's not what you assume it is. It wasn't a sentence. He was giving me time. No, not that sort of time! And if that's still more confusing, please allow me to explain.

We had recently moved to Nottingham from Eastbourne with an offer of employment with a new company. We bought a house in Calverton, a former mining village on the north of the city. I took a mortgage on the property, a fairly high percentage mortgage on the strength of the income. It was 1989 and the economy was in bad shape. The firm I worked for went bust and I had a mortgage to pay, there were few people that we knew, a village with no employment opportunities and we had a family with three dependent children. The interest rate had risen to 15%. I took immediate self employment sales work in order to keep the family fed and the bills paid but the mortgage had already got behind with the loss of the regular income.

The bank decided it was time to reclaim the house, that's why I was in court that day.

Properties weren't selling, prices were dropping, we weren't in the city where there was more potential for jobs and house sales, however, after praying we had a strong sense that God was in control of this situation and that we would find a buyer for the house swiftly, that we wouldn't lose out financially, or our name and credit rating brought into any disrepute.

It was a simple closed courtroom. I walked in with faith and confidence and announced that if we could be granted two months, the house would be sold and the bank would be repaid in full.

I can only recall it as a smug kind of snigger at my foolish ignorance that came from the two bank representatives. 'Nothing is selling - there's no point. We want full possession in one month.' As I said before, we got three. The magistrate was not impressed at the attitude of the bank, saw the hope in my eyes and knowing that a house sale normally took three months, minimum, gave me that time. Just in case.

The house was marketed. That week people came and looked at it, offered full asking price and we had the quickest sale I have ever known, and as many of our friends know, we have sold a lot of properties, either as investors or in home moves!

The house was vacant in five weeks from that court hearing, the bank repaid in full and God provided us a flat rental in a very sought after location after jumping us to the top of a big waiting list for this property.

We had space and time to reassess, rebuild and restore our lives.

I won't go into detail here about how we managed to leapfrog a prior list of prospective tenants, or indeed how God miraculously restored a broken down car and how it drove as if it had been made new again, but suffice to say, when we come to the end of our own resources and there are no more answers in the natural, that's the moment God can act. He loves it when we recognise him as our only hope and I can almost hear him say, 'move over my son, it's my time now...'

Help Us Lord...

I recall running out of sand many years ago now. It was quite important. My wife and I had a shop, and a builder and I were concreting the floor late on a Saturday so that we could reopen on the Monday. We had worked back and almost reached the door when the sand ran out. We had cement and water, but no sand. If it had been the other end, behind the counter say, not so much of a problem, but with no trades open on a Sunday back then and needing not to have a weak point by the door, as well as Gary going back to work on the Monday, we really wanted to finish the job. This was a 'help us Lord' situation. We stood in the doorway looking in and prayed for a miracle 'of loaves and fishes' asking God to increase our sand. No sooner had we said our 'amen' - I do not lie, a voice from behind asked, 'is there a problem; can I help?' We explained our situation and he said, 'come with me'. He had parked up outside the shop and had a van. He opened the doors at the back and I looked into an empty van. I thought. That was until my eyes focused on the wonderful layer of golden building sand spread out across the floor of the van. That was it, apart from the broom with which he shovelled it out before going on his way.

Do you normally come through here at this time I had asked inquisitively? No he replied, I usually take the main road past, but I just happened to come this way today and parked up outside your shop. Amazing! How does God orchestrate such a complex situation? I have no idea but I'm happy that he can! We cranked up the cement mixer and the job was done. This is very good for building faith as well as building floors!

No need for a 'mind the gap' sign to placed by the door for the customers the following week.

God's time zone is not chronological like ours. He doesn't wake up each morning and reach for the daily prayer list. He has heard your prayer, past, present and future. He is the Omniscient God, all knowing, and of course ever present and ever powerful.

C. S. Lewis remarks: '[God] has all eternity in which to listen to the split second of prayer put up by a pilot as his plane crashes in flames.'[11]

This should lead us into such a sense of trust; that God has and always is listening to our prayers, and our cries of despair and 'help me Lord'.

Just remember the first miracle of Jesus at the wedding of Cana. The wine was gone, resources were run dry, literally. The cry of Mary was; 'help us Lord'. Jesus didn't just replace the wine; he made the best wine you could ever taste. If the guests had run out, they had probably drunk too much already, but they could still taste that the good wine was now even better than before.

God doesn't simply replace, he renews, your mind, your soul, your spirit, your faith.

In the court the magistrate had become my advocate. He was of course the 'judge' over the matter also, but in a sense he stood in the gap, in mediating the situation between us, and those with whom we had to pay and maintain a formerly agreed contract.

Jesus of course goes much further than the earthly mediator. He truly stands in the gap and he pays the price of what we owe. We approach the Father with the old house of sin and failure, sold and vacant, and invite him to the new house of our heart where he can take up residence.

He's always ready, as the atoning sacrifice of our Lord has made possible, to walk with us, live in us and work on our behalf, to make the impossible possible and the supernatural natural.

John said in his letter: 'My dear children, I write this to you so that you will not sin. But if anybody does sin, we have an advocate with the Father - Jesus Christ, the Righteous One. He is the atoning sacrifice for our sins, and not only for ours but also for the sins of the whole world' (1 John 2:1-2).

We touched on atonement in the first section, how there was a 'covering' of atonement in the Old Covenant, and how we now enjoy the fulfilment of the remittance of our sins and failings through the New Covenant, established in Jesus through his sacrifice.

Jesus tells a parable in Luke 16. He speaks of Lazarus, a poor man who has died and now sits in a Heavenly place with Abraham by his side. The rich man also dies but finds himself in hades, tormented and looking up at the poor man. How he wished he had done more for the poor man while he was alive. How he wished that he had recognised his need to humble himself before God while he was alive. He asks for the poor man to come and comfort him but he cannot, as Abraham says: '...there is a great chasm separating us. No one can cross over to you from here, and no one can cross over to us from there' (Luke 16:26, NLT). The gap is too great. Only miraculous intervention can ever close the gap. Only the cross of Jesus can span the chasm.

The Old Testament was always *'mind the gap'* but the excellent, amazing builder and joiner of the New Testament has beautifully filled the gap and joined us together with the Father, and in him we have our whole being. 'To Jesus the mediator of a new covenant, and to the sprinkled blood that speaks a better word than the blood of Abel' (Heb 12:24).

Hebrews chapters 7 and 8 in detail demonstrate how Jesus has mediated a New Covenant for us that no longer only covers us, but cleanses us from all sin, not just for a moment in time but for all time. He is a priest forever in the order of Melchizedek, of whom there is some debate on whether he was a human King of Jerusalem, an Angel or the pre-figured manifestation of The Son of God. What we do know is that Melchizedek, 'king of righteousness' pre-dates the Levitical system of priesthood, appearing in Gen 14, where Abraham paid him homage and was both presented with bread and wine, and blessed. Jesus, like Melchizedek who is not of the Levite system, 'outdates' the old system of priesthood, and we are free to enjoy the blessing of the Lord and remember his covenant, in the remembrance of his body through the taking of the bread and wine in communion.

In John 17, Jesus is essentially fulfilling the role of the high priest in his prayer to the Father on our behalf. He is preparing for the sacrificial atonement of his own life.

The Old Testament priests were anointed to act as temporary mediators between man and God. Advocates, on behalf of the guilt of the people, until Jesus came as the ultimate and final High Priest.

There is much about the anointing of God throughout scriptures, briefly there was:

The leper's anointing that came with healing and spoke of salvation from sin.

The priestly anointing that speaks of the body of Christ, the church together as ministers of the gospel.

The Kingly anointing of obedience and reign: for us in Christ through his sacrifice.

The prophetic anointing that guides us and speaks truth and encouragement.

All of these 'anointings' are bestowed freely upon us as recipients of the advocacy of Christ on our behalf.

We have come to our great High Priest with our 'leprosy' healed, all of our sin gone, and he has declared us both whole and holy.

We are now part of the body of Christ; we are all priests and ambassadors in his name as we represent him.

We stand as kings before him and before the enemy, and will reign with him in all eternity.

His Spirit lives within us, and leaves in us the deposit of faith and the seed of his perfect nature.

In the last days of the Tsars, I have heard it said, although I haven't referenced this myself, that Tsar Alexander would disguise himself and go secretly at night to see how the troops were coping. He came across one soldier, drunk, passed out and in distress. He owed a great deal of money. He had scribbled the amount on a piece of paper with the words, 'Who will pay?' - Tsar Alexander simply wrote, 'I will pay...Alexander'.

My advocate has paid in full. He has atoned for my sins. He has mediated salvation on my behalf. Glory! Like the defeated soldier, all I have to do is to approach the Throne of Grace, and accept the offer and receive the mercy of the anointed one, The King of Kings, and the Lord of Lords. The price has been paid.

Chapter 11.

GRACE AND GRATEFULNESS –
Apply Daily

Credit or Debit?

We took our seats in the 1000 strong congregation on the Sunday morning at the Albert Hall in Nottingham. The church had outgrown its current premises, which was also being used as a Christian school, and was renting this lovely building and filling it weekly. For us this was to be no ordinary Sunday morning.

Bananas And Legs...

Part of the way through the service David Shearman, Pastor and lead elder of the church took the microphone and with slight hesitation he asked, 'Is there someone here with an aversion to bananas?' A little nudge from my wife and I indicated - yes. 'Stand up' he said and with some reluctance I stood. I looked round to see how many others were on their feet. After all I can't be the only one, surely. But I was. That's one way for God to get your attention. David's concerns assuaged, he confidently prophesied over me that God was standing with us and that he had a special plan for my life. It was very specific even though it seems that the plan is still a work in progress. There was a moment of hesitation and then God spoke to David further. 'Is there something wrong with your legs?' He asked. No, I answered but there is something wrong with Carole's. He then prophesied further that Carole would not end up in a wheelchair. You have to think here, as he confessed to us later that evening, 'If I get this wrong I really am going to look silly. *Bananas and Legs!*' All the other leaders were sitting behind him, common practice at that time and 'the word of the Lord was rare in those days' to quote scripture. Actually it wasn't really so rare, but such prophetic messages weren't being constantly given in those services if memory serves. And if this weird one was wrong, maybe his position might be on the line here, he confessed to us later that evening!

At this point we didn't fully understand the enormity of what was to come but he was so right. He had clearly heard from God. Bananas? Horrid things! (To me) Difficult times? Just round the corner. What I wrote in the previous chapter about the house was soon to occur, and God was preparing us, raising our faith level so that we would stand in the day of trouble with full assurance that God was walking right there with us, and would make a way where there seemed to be no way.

Engaging with the grace of God and experiencing it is so valuable. You see grace isn't a dormant state. Grace is active. It is enabling us and living in us.

Grace is unmerited, unearned divine favour. It is divine enablement and is free at the point of contact with no hidden charges later on.

Grace has been freely credited into our account. Abraham believed God and it was credited to him as righteousness, but sin still put a debit on the account and the debit was always greater than the credit, which hopefully is not the case in your bank account today! Paul In Rom 4 tells us that we too are credited righteousness as Jesus was 'delivered over to death for our sins and was raised to life for our justification' v.25.

We stand before God, righteous, our account is always in credit because righteousness is imputed to our account. This Grace is unchanging and unending, and of course we need it to be so!

It was just a couple of years after the prophecy that Sunday when Carole suffered a total physical breakdown. There had been signs. From the late 70's there was a partial loss of sight for a short period. There were pins and needles that rose from her feet to her neck that came and went without a diagnosis.

It was August 1992 when Carole fell several times at work. One night she woke with terrible pain in her head and ear and in the morning was unable to stand. The doctor who came diagnosed a prolapsed disc and prescribed bed rest. However the dizziness and pain grew worse and I took Carole to the surgery where she worked. The GP sent her immediately to Queens Medical Centre in Nottingham. She was there for 5 days unable to move or to function properly. Any lights or noise were a real problem and were greatly amplified in her head. I worked early each morning and spent the rest of the day at the bedside.

She had an MRI scan and the results soon were verified. It was Multiple Sclerosis.

She improved sufficiently to continue working for the next few years until the symptoms would come more frequently, and by 1995, with more and more time off work she decided to resign from her job.

The practice where Carole worked lent us a wheelchair for times when she couldn't walk. There would be occasions when she would literally crawl up the stairs to bed in our cottage in Linby.

About this time, 'The Christian Channel' began to be aired on TV, and Carole quickly engaged with this and the powerful messages of faith and healing that were broadcast, to the exclusion of most, if not all of the other 'day time' TV programmes.

Writing down things that we had not really heard before in this depth, and seeking God in prayer began to build a positive faith filled attitude in the mind of Carole. I would return from work and she would be in praise or in the word and believing for healing.

We listened to Kenneth Copeland's inspired messages of faith and the healing ministry of people like Benny Hinn, and simply believed the word of God that we were hearing.

It is the mind that must be renewed, and 'rewired' spiritually that enables such a strong connection with God. It is the mind that houses the brain, our will and our emotions. As I write, this is exactly what Dr Caroline Leaf has been talking about in a daily programme with Kenneth and Gloria Copeland on TBN just now.

How science is proving scripture and scripture is proving science is remarkable.

The movie *The Farewell* is based on a true-life story about an 80 year old grandmother of a family in China, who has been diagnosed with stage 4 lung cancer. It appears that in China, a diagnosis is given to family members and not directly to the patient. It is for the family to decide what should be shared. They decide to keep it a secret for as long as possible, and meanwhile all the family from America and China come to visit under the guise of a family wedding. Of course they have really come to say 'goodbye'. The story develops around a debate of whether they should be honest or continue the pretence, until one of them states: 'In China there is a saying; "it's not the cancer that kills you, it's the fear."'

Now that is quite a revealing statement. Although medical science might not endorse that as a fact, it is nevertheless true that both spiritually and physically, fear has a huge effect in the mind and on the body. A 'fact' is not always a 'truth'.

The *fact* is that there is an enemy of our salvation and our healing, who likes nothing better than using our fear as his playground to wreak havoc in our lives.

The *truth* is that there is one who has taken that fear and despair, in His body on the cross, in order to bring us hope and joy, freedom, salvation, health and blessing.

(Remarkably, or perhaps not so; 6 years after her terminal diagnosis, according to the movie, the Chinese Grandmother is still living!)

Returning to our own story, we saw that there was to be a trip to Israel for ten days in September of 1996, a 'Benny Hinn' organised event, and so much we wanted to go. In fact we were determined to go. I phoned up to check if it was ok to bring a wheelchair, and could we get around in a wheelchair? All the while mindful of the prophetic word, 'you will never end up in a wheelchair'.

Previous to this trip there was to be meeting at Earls Court in London in August, with Benny Hinn and team. The worship was really powerfully anointed and one of the team, a lovely lady came along our row, particularly as this was for those in wheelchairs. She stopped in front of Carole and began praying and speaking healing, that 'by his wounds you have been healed'. She pulled her from the wheelchair and in that moment, the active grace of God overcame that curse of disease and Carole began walking and then running up and down the aisle.

We rejoiced as we left that meeting and Carole felt free of the debilitating effect of the disease. However as we travelled she sensed a return of the nerve pain in her leg. This aside we returned the wheelchair to the GP practice knowing that healing had come.

We went to Israel and Carole walked miles all around the streets of Jerusalem, Capernaum, Masada and the Dead Sea, a superb meal at the Sea of Galilee, free of the MS with clear physical evidence of her healing, and so grateful for the grace and the embrace of the Father. That is irreplaceable.

It was a wonderful time of walking where Jesus walked, amazing times of worship and the word, organised as only Americans can. A 5 Star trip with incredible hotels, meticulously chosen for the choicest food and ambience, all planned to perfection.

There were 2 coaches for the English and a whole lot more for the Americans!

Carole's brother had recently become a Christian following the death of their dad, and at the last minute he came too. Our daughter Becci was also with us at age 13. We had been baptised but not Richard at this point. On the final day everyone took the 'Jordan experience' of being baptised in the river with all robes provided. 'As a symbol.' We were in the first group, as ours was the earlier plane home to the UK and Benny Hinn symbolically baptised the first groups. Carole, Becci and I went through and then Richard. Suddenly Benny Hinn kept hold of Richard. 'Hold it' he said, 'this one is for real'. He again baptised Richard in a more meaningful way. He had no prior knowledge of Richard's recent conversion, only the testimony of God in his spirit. A wonderful place to be actually baptised in water!

Today? Carole remains free of the disease of MS but continues to live with the damage that was caused to the nerves. She hasn't had steroids or scans for many years now, but still has to live with a certain amount of pain and numbness in the leg. Her healing means that she is able to take care of the driving duties all the while I am not permitted to do so, until that restriction is lifted – (which is now the case as I edit this book).

I realise that sometimes the flamboyant styles of what can be seen as 'superstar' preachers will not be to everyone's taste, but remember that everyone begins their walk in humility, and we should all be attempting to continue to walk humbly before the Lord, and as such, not judging others.

I would say that for me, I am not in a position to 'cast the first stone!' Nor would I want to. What is true is that you can't box God in to our particular way of thinking.

John the Baptist was, I guess, the superstar of his generation, drawing crowds in with his very unorthodox lifestyle, his weird diet and genuine camel jacket. But he taught about the Messiah and that's what is important.

God heals in multiple ways. I have always suffered badly with hay fever and then I began to struggle with asthma. My doctor was a specialist and told me that one can develop from the other, that the two can be linked. Struggling for breath if I exerted myself and using an inhaler, a friend noticed this. He is a man of faith, who on becoming a Christian sold his business for a pound, and has lived by faith writing Bible teaching courses to train leaders across the world how to teach new believers, and also how they can develop their own local economies. He himself had been instantly and miraculously healed from asthma and he simply laid hands on me and spoke healing over that respiratory issue. I have never used that inhaler again and when the summer came around there was no more hay fever either. God heals if there are two thousand or just two.

Keep on reaching out to the Father despite how the circumstances appear. He is always bigger and greater than the mountain in front of you. Speak by faith and cast it away.

Yes it all sounds very simple to speak to the mountain and it will be cast into the sea, but Jesus is really trying to teach his disciples that there is no mountain, or no obstacle that is greater than God. He is above every earthly circumstance, and every battle has to be won in the realm of the spirit, both through and by the sovereignty of God.

The battle is out there, but the battle is The Lord's. With this understanding we must rebuke every evil work that the enemy forges against us, and we must resist all of his endeavours to undermine our covenant of blessing, through the mighty name of Jesus.

We must live by faith in the word of God. Walking daily in Grace, Salvation and Healing. Remember that our account is always in credit. Satan can have the debit. He's not coming into our house. We are eternally grateful for all that the Father has done, is doing and will continue to do. Speak with me these words of faith and truth and declare in every situation and circumstance: His Kingdom Come.

As for me and my house, we will serve the Lord.
(Josh 24:15, KJV)

Chapter 12.

THE SHEPHERD AND THE SHEEP –
Fully Forgiven

The Lord is my Shepherd - I have all that I need.
Ps 23 (NLT)

I walked past the headmaster's office to the familiar 'thwacking' sound. The year. 1966. The place. St Mary's boys school, Eastbourne. I glanced across at the flight of stone stairs, where those of us brave enough would run, leap and throw ourselves from the top to the bottom in our 'time challenge' game. 'Risking life and limb and if surviving that - the hangman's noose.' Well, the headmaster's cane to be honest. If caught.

In my time at the school I was only sentenced to the cane on one occasion, which was commuted to the slipper at trial, and administered by one of the kinder 'school masters' who had little appetite for corporal punishment. I had heard of regular offenders who would keep a little book in their shorts to reduce the effect of the cane on the bottom, but I can't verify this!

I joined this school by virtue of the fact that we had moved house. In my former school I mainly recall being forced to eat the dreaded bowl of bananas and custard despite my protestations. 'On your own head (or feet) be it' I thought, as they stood over me and of course I promptly threw it back up over their shoes and the floor. Apart from this, it seemed a fairly 'easy going' school.

St Mary's however ran on military lines with military precision. Perhaps some of the teachers had served in the war and brought their ideas of authority and discipline with them. (I am being generous here.)

On my first day assembling in the playground I had no idea what was going on. At the sound of **'Attention'** all the boys suddenly 'fell in' saluting the head in their neat groups. I was left standing in no mans land and quite bemused.

What are you doing boy, get into your regiment! He bellowed. I picked a group and 'fell in' mumbling 'yes sir…'

One day some boys took my cap off me. I was horrified. To turn up at school without a cap, could lead to expulsion, if not execution!

Then there was Mr Clear. He could lift a boy up by the ears, place him on his desk, tell the class to 'look at this boy' and then deftly knock him off again. Fascinating!

Then the time came to move on from primary education into the big league.

My secondary school made a valiant attempt at providing an education. The woodwork master was incredibly adept at throwing small blocks of wood at children's heads, and the sports master might punch a boy to the ground if he dared offered a 'please excuse me' sick note! He delighted in taking us for 'Shinty' - (Now only played by Scottish brave hearts) - a wild and fearsome game, where a ball would fly agonisingly at any height, and hockey sticks would swing at both shins and shoulders. 'A skilful eye and a sense of survival are paramount' says the rule book!

The science master could gleefully 'electrocute' the entire class at once. 'All hold hands and hold this cable' he quipped as he plugged us in.

Playground spot checks were made to measure hair length and flare width. Suspension could result.

The head took us for English literature one day, the door opened and in he crawled, on all fours and barking like a dog...

It was around this time, that I had an overwhelming sense that this may not have been the best choice of school after all, nor perhaps the best years of my life....

Why are you telling us all this silly nonsense you may well ask, and you would be right to wonder why? I realise that I am presenting my early and formative years of authority figures in a comical way, and many of your experiences may not be a laughing matter. We all live with authority over us, be it parenting, education, employment, relationship, retirement, judgemental and governmental, and every experience is different. They shape our past, our present and our future. In worldly terms we call this fate. 'Que sera, sera, whatever will be will be' as the song goes. As believers we live under a different authority in which we declare our eternal hope in God, and the certainty of our eternal destiny and his hand of protection over every area of our lives. 'For in him we live and move and have our being' (Acts 17:28a). With His authority given freely to us, we have the *right* to determine the destination. We live by faith, not by fate. He is always greater than any goliath that attempts to defy His purpose in us, and we know and proclaim that our Heavenly Father is sovereign over us.

My own father was a good father, as you may have guessed from the car incident.

I recall the excitement of eagerly anticipating the little box of Lego every Friday when dad came home from work. I also recall the times when we weren't on the same page. My increasing hair length and hopeless attempts to persuade him that King Crimson, Genesis and Yes, were really just a progressive rock extension to his classical music, fell on deaf ears. Frustration on both sides was inevitable as he was far more of a 'Mozart' man than a 'Stravinsky' man, and therefore the gulf was too great!

In our own *'mind the gap'* scenario, as a woodwind player, I found it much easier to cross the bridge over to loving classical music than he could do so in my direction.

Perhaps he would 'air conduct' to a Beethoven symphony but I don't remember him ever playing 'air guitar' to a Zeppelin LP or rocking out with Wishbone Ash' 'jail bait!' Possibly even 'Bridge over troubled water' was a bridge too far to cross....

(As time passed however, we did begin to appreciate each other's tastes far better.)

All of this aside, I was constantly aware of his loving kindness as a father to his children, and a husband to my mother.

From the testimonies that provoked the writing of this book, to seeing the struggle in many lives, I am fully aware that not everyone has experienced an upbringing with a really good father. Perhaps your experience is that of an unloving father, or a father trying to cope with his own difficulties, or maybe simply an absent or abusive father.

Then again, having a poor experience with your own mother can lead to the same destiny of distrust in *any* authority that declares 'you are valuable and loved'.

Strangely, I would rather go to mum when I had done wrong than dad, as I had an expectation that she would mediate on my behalf. At these times it would seem that he was 'head of the house' and his authority would be absolute. Possibly because of the authority figures in my daily schooling, it felt that dad would be less immediately approachable.

With the Lord Jesus and our Heavenly Father, this may well also be how we react, but we need to remember again that Jesus has paid once and for all, for all of our sin, so that we can come straight to the Throne of Grace. The curtain of separation has been torn down.

We may often view mothers as having more compassion than fathers, but although this is often true, it is not always the case. God gives us a wonderful picture in Isaiah 49:15-16b. 'Can a woman forget her nursing child, that she should have no compassion on the son of her womb? Even these may forget, yet I will not forget you. Behold, I have engraved you on the palms of my hand.'

God is not only a Father to us, but is as a Mother who is *full* of compassion.

Despite how much our emotions are lifted or damaged by earthly experience, in either case our view is clouded, because just as the worst father imaginable is as far from perfect as imaginable, so the best father imaginable would be far from perfect in his humanity alone, apart from in the renewing of his spirit through the redemptive power of Jesus.

Even then, only the character of the Heavenly Father can be truly viewed as perfect, all embracing in his holiness and continually reaching out to his children with a love that is beyond measure.

The Lord Is My Shepherd...

Through Jesus we can truly say with David that 'The Lord is my Shepherd'.

Many Scriptures speak of the Lord being our Shepherd and we being his sheep. The truth is, not many of us today have a clear understanding of the role of the Shepherd in Bible times. Not surprising, as many of us live in towns and cities, and those in the business are more inclined to consider themselves as sheep farmers, and it seems a world away in time and place; But not to the people in Bible days.

All I knew of shepherds I had learned on 'One man and his dog!' With a Yorkshire man whistling weirdly and crying out 'come-bye...' in his Yorkshire drawl! I really think that this probably had little in common to the understanding of the Shepherd and the sheep in the beautiful Psalm 23, or the words of Jesus in John 10, and many other references.

In those days being a shepherd was a lowly position: A menial, tough and despised job in the terrain of the Middle East. Indeed, a shepherd would be looked down upon as a person less than adequate to hold any position of honour or merit.

The angels appeared first to announce Jesus' birth to shepherds. Considered as harshly as outlaws, many not to be trusted and of little worth, God was showing us that he was *showing up* in order to represent you and me in the court of heaven.

Yet Jesus refers to himself as a Shepherd. 'The Good Shepherd.' One whose sheep would know his voice and follow his lead. He warns against the 'hireling shepherd'. The agency shepherd who was interested only in his own wellbeing and not that of those he was charged to look after. At the first sign of trouble he would bolt and leave the sheep lost and without hope or protection.

Jesus says that he is the only Good Shepherd to rely upon, because he is prepared to lay down his life and that he has the authority to lay it down and to take it up again, speaking of his death and resurrection.

'I am the gate for the sheep' Jesus said in John 10:7. A shepherd would lie down in the opening of the sheep pen and effectively become both the gate of protection for the sheep against wolf or thief, and also the gate of entry to come in and go out, freely, under the cover of the shepherd, and find pasture.

There are many voices that say 'try this way' or 'open this gate' - 'who needs God anyway?' but inevitly they lead to loss, being lost, and in lack of that good pasture.

The Good Shepherd is under authority to look out for the sheep and that authority he uses wisely as he safely guides his flock. He doesn't bark at them, he isn't waiting to take out his frustrations upon them, he doesn't get angry with them or punish them. He cares for them and knows them by name.

The sheep are hopeless without the shepherd as we are hopeless without God. On the TV news just last night I saw a story that involved sheep being mutilated and killed by a couple of dogs. There was nothing they could do on their own, even if there were many more of their number than their attackers. They're just not 'wired' that way. And neither are we. Without God we stand without the protection of his grace and at the mercy of whatever the enemy desires to throw at us.

A thousand years before the birth of Jesus, David wrote his songs of praise and worship, of prophecy of the coming Messiah and of deliverance. He lived a life of a shepherd and a King, in the light of his love for God. Did he know Jesus? Perhaps not like the apostle John who lived in his physical presence, and yet intuitively in his spirit he displays and describes the Saviour in the Father. The Holy Spirit reveals the inseparable truth of the trinity.

In Psalm 103 he urges his soul to praise the Lord with all of his being, not to forget all his benefits, that he forgives sins, heals disease, redeems and crowns us with love and compassion. He satisfies our desires, renews us, he doesn't treat us as we deserve. As high as are the heavens, so high is his love for us. As far as the east is from the west he has removed our transgressions. Beyond measure. This is the Father who has compassion on his children.

Recently I was wondering, 'Father, when your Son was brutally crucified did you suffer?' Is there a sense in which as we think of the words of Jesus, 'My God, my God, why have you forsaken me' that we assume that God somehow just took the weekend off?

While I was pondering this, my daughter had come in to the house one evening in the dark, and bending down she struck her face on a chair just below her right eye. The skin was cut and it bled, but didn't develop any further under her eye. However the following day I awoke with a black eye! I had a big bruise under my right eye. The next day it was worse. I went to see the doctor who was puzzled, as I had not struck my eye and nothing had flown into it. 'I'm not sure what it can be' he said. He thought of antibiotics but decided to 'wait and see'. I had never had a black eye before and just felt that God was showing me that when his Son died, he too suffered. Now I can't make a theology out of this, but nevertheless it was I believe a poignant moment.

When my daughter was just 2 years old, I remember sitting with her cuddling up to me while we watched 'Winnie the Pooh' on TV. It was a beautiful moment that I wont forget. I felt such love and compassion for my little girl that I knew I would do anything for her. If she were to suffer I knew that I would feel the pain of that too. This is a small and inadequate picture of how both Jesus and the Father felt on that momentous day.

Here is a similar situation that Benny Hinn experienced as his son slept in his arms.

'I felt an overwhelming outpouring of unquenchable love for my son.

While I continued to stroke his head gently, basking in the beauty of the priceless moment, the Lord whispered, "What are your feelings toward your son right now?"

Although I recognised His still, small voice, I was startled by the question. Again the gentle voice of the

Master said softly, "Can you describe what you are feeling right now?"

I struggled to find the right words and finally replied, "No Master, I can't begin to put it into words. The depth and dimension of my love for my son are beyond description."

"Benny," the Lord said, "What you are feeling can't even be compared to the love I have for you. It's only a tiny drop in the ocean by comparison. It's a weak and worldly example of what I feel toward you. My love for you is so full of kindness – My kindness so full of love. My love is steadfast, unselfish, unchangeable, and endless. My love for you never, ever fails."

In that tender moment, as I held my sleeping child in my arms, the love that I felt as a father was so rich. But as the Lord spoke to my heart, comparing the love I felt toward Joshua with the greatness of His tender love for me, I understood how weak and frail my love for my son was when compared to God the Father's infinite love for us, His children.' [12]

Perhaps David knew the depth of God's love in a deeper way than any other person throughout the Bible. From his poetry and songs in the Psalms, we read of his devotion to God in every circumstance that he faced, the longing for His love and kindness, His justice and mercy, and he recognised the Father's devotion to him despite his many failings and times of waywardness. Regarding such an intimacy with the Father, maybe it would be appropriate for us to summarise each chapter of our journey of 'Embracing the Father' through the picture of this wonderful and most recognised psalm of David...

PSALM 23.

THE LORD IS MY SHEPHERD
The Lover and the Loved

The Good Shepherd that Jesus talks about in John 10 knows the sheep and they know him. He knows them by name and they follow him because they know his voice. A wise sheep doesn't follow any voice. If the sheep is lost, if we are lost, the Good Shepherd will come searching until he finds him, because he cares deeply for him, or her.

I LACK NOTHING
Creation and Curse

Created to live in the blessing of an all Loving Father. Just as sheep would have no cause of fear, so in the perfect love of God, our fear is cast out and we have no despair. The curse against us has been lifted. He provides us with all that we need. In his presence we want for nothing.

HE MAKES ME LIE DOWN IN GREEN PASTURES
Running and Rescue

In desert climes, just as the shepherd would always be seeking good pasture to feed his sheep, in the tough terrain of negotiating life so God loves to rescue us in order that we can live under his covenant of continual grace. 'For it is by grace you have been saved, through faith, and this not from ourselves, it is the gift of God, not by works so that no one can boast' (Eph 2:8-9).

HE LEADS ME BESIDE QUIET WATERS
Rebellion and Redemption

Sheep can be stubborn by nature, and even quite rebellious like we humans are. A friend who farms sheep confirmed this. I was surprised, but then my cat once he is determined to sleep in a particular spot cannot be dissuaded. He whines miserably until he gets his own way. We also want to go our own way, and in our sinful nature are rebellious people, as those in the days of Noah. We need a Shepherd who will hold us, and redeem us, before we end up drowning in the 'flood waters' that sweep us away.

HE REFRESHES MY SOUL
Blessing and Belonging

He refreshes and revives us instead, in those quiet and peaceful waters that he provides. It's a special feeling to know that you belong somewhere or to someone. God never chose the proud, the arrogant, the strong, the bold or the wealthy. He looks for the heart, yielded to him, the lowly, 'the nobody', the weak, the fearful and the poor. Just to raise us up in his blessing and restore us with his presence.

HE GUIDES ME ALONG THE RIGHT PATHS FOR HIS NAME'S SAKE
Sin and Sanctification

In restoration we remain in right relationship with the Father. He guides us; He leads us. He clears the way ahead like the shepherd does for the sheep. He wants the sheep to remain close so they don't get caught up in the brambles off the path. Neither do we need to be caught up in the entanglement of life outside of his guidance, by drifting off the path he has made for us. He has made a way through the wilderness.

EVEN THOUGH I WALK THROUGH THE DARKEST VALLEY, I WILL FEAR NO EVIL
Faith and Faithfulness

Sometimes the valley has to be negotiated before the mountain can be climbed.

This is a time to look up. Perhaps for the shepherd it was when the sheep were attacked or their environment raged against them. This is a time to remember who we are in Christ, fear has no place; in the darkest times, remaining faithful overcomes all that rages against us. In the testimony we look forward, no turning back...

FOR YOU ARE WITH ME, YOUR ROD AND YOUR STAFF, THEY COMFORT ME
Judgement and Justice

The shepherd stood in front of the sheep. He led his sheep; he didn't drive them from behind. He stood, the first in line to defend them against the enemy with his rod of protection, and to discipline them with his staff of comfort. He gently 'hooks' the sheep and brings them back as they stray. Our Shepherd stands in front of us too. He lays down his life for the sheep. Our judgement is upon him. Like sheep we have done nothing to deserve anything, but receive everything.

YOU PREPARE A TABLE BEFORE ME IN THE PRESENCE OF MY ENEMIES
Rest and Restoration

'A table' in the geological sense of the word would be a plateau. Whether you consider that this is the intention here, or the usual transcription of 'the banqueting table' (and both are valid expressions), the general tenor is that the shepherd provides a safe place. A place of restoration: Higher ground and a fresh perspective: No longer in the valley looking up. The Shepherd feeds us with his word. He loves us with his passion, and protects us in the presence of opposition, as we rest in his presence.

YOU ANOINT MY HEAD WITH OIL. MY CUP OVERFLOWS
Atonement and Advocacy

Here the shepherd anoints the sheep. He pours the oil on the head so that the insects and reptiles can't attack. Our Shepherd is anointed so that we too can receive the anointing of the Holy Spirit. The cup of anointing overflowed. Jesus received that anointing of perfume before making atonement on our behalf: By the priest? No, by the one despised and of no value. What an advocate! Perfect acceptance. My cup truly overflows with joy, just as the wine overflowed at that wedding...

SURELY GOODNESS AND LOVE WILL FOLLOW ME ALL THE DAYS OF MY LIFE
Grace and Gratefulness

He's always on the look out. The Shepherd, that is. He leads the sheep and they follow. In his great grace we find that not only does the Father lead us by the Spirit but he is our rear guard too. His goodness, his mercy and love follow us every step we take. Yes, I'm so grateful for grace.

AND I WILL DWELL IN THE HOUSE OF THE LORD FOR EVER
The Shepherd and the Sheep

Stay under the anointing. Dwell in his house. Don't wander off. He's a good Father. The thief comes only to steal and destroy. God comes to offer life to the full. Compassionate. Slow to anger, abounding in mercy. His authority over us safeguards us, because it is motivated by his perfect love and forgiveness. Forever.

CONCLUSION

In a survey in America by evangelist Mark Rutland, according to Philip Yancey, people were asked what words they most like to hear. The first he predicted.

'I love you.' Number two was 'I forgive you.' The third choice took him by surprise: 'Supper's ready.'

Rutland realised that these three responses give a summary to the gospel, loved by God, forgiven by God and invited to the banquet table.[13]

It appears that in an unstable world of uncertainty, the world is actually prioritising what God has intended all along. We are created by a loving God; He who steps into our world so that nothing can separate us from his love that permeates our entire being, and so wonderfully embraces us.

Take a moment to read here the testimony of David, as he escapes from the attack of Abimelech on his life, and prompts us to testify likewise:

I bless God every chance I get.
My lungs expand with his praise.
I live and breathe God. If things aren't going well,
hear this and be happy.

Join me in spreading the news.
Together let's get the word out.
God met me more than halfway.
He freed me from my anxious fears.

Look at him and give him your warmest smile.
Never hide your feelings from him.

When I was desperate I called out and
God got me out of a tight spot.
God's angel sets up a circle of protection
around us while we pray.

Open your mouth and taste, open
your eyes and see how good God is.
Blessed are you who run to him.

Worship God if you want the best.
Worship opens doors to all his goodness.
(Psalm 34:1-9, The Message Translation)

Going through a time of trial and tribulation can often bring a cloud of doubt and uncertainty, like a mist that blocks out the sun. Looking back in the light of his glory however, demonstrates how God has weaved together a plan and a purpose to free us from the past, our anxious fears and those 'tight spots' that we often find ourselves in. His arms of protection are always holding us.

We closed the first section with verses from 1 John chapter 4.

In conclusion of 'Embracing the Father'- reading a little further now in this chapter, we find these amazing truths that John has written in his letter.

If anyone acknowledges that Jesus is the Son of God, God lives in them and they in God. And so we know and rely on the love God has for us.

God is love. Whoever lives in love lives in God, and God in them.

This is how love is made complete among us so that we will have confidence on the day of judgement: in this world we are like Jesus.

There is no fear in love. But perfect love drives out fear, because fear has to do with punishment. The one who fears is not made perfect in love.

We love because he first loved us. (1 John 4:15-19)

...REFLECTION...

Does God love us more because of Jesus? Does he love us more because of the cross?

Has he come round to a new way of thinking because of what Jesus has done for us?

Of course not! I hope that I have been able to demonstrate that The Father has *purposed* that he has, and always will love his children, and longs for all of us to find the greatness and wonder of such love.

He has set out to love us from the very beginning and will do so for all eternity.

Even before he made the world, God loved us and chose us in Christ to be holy and without fault in his eyes. (Eph 1:4, NLT)

This is sacrificial love. This is the deep, Father's love that pours itself out, undiluted and unsolicited. This is Agape love. Often unsought or requested, yet constantly offered to all who seek, that they may find. So today, why not seek, why not find?

We love you Lord for who you are and what you have accomplished for us. Lead us we pray to know you more clearly, more dearly and more intimately.

So embrace the Father today. After all,
he's reaching out to embrace you.

HOW DEEP THE FATHER'S LOVE FOR US

HOW DEEP THE FATHER'S LOVE FOR US
HOW VAST BEYOND ALL MEASURE
THAT HE SHOULD GIVE HIS ONLY SON
TO MAKE A WRETCH HIS TREASURE
HOW GREAT THE PAIN OF SEARING LOSS
THE FATHER TURNS HIS FACE AWAY
AS WOUNDS WHICH MAR THE CHOSEN ONE
BRING MANY SONS TO GLORY

BEHOLD THE MAN UPON THE CROSS
MY SIN UPON HIS SHOULDERS
ASHAMED I HEAR MY MOCKING VOICE
CALL OUT AMONG THE SCOFFERS
IT WAS MY SIN THAT HELD HIM THERE
UNTIL IT WAS ACCOMPLISHED
HIS DYING BREATH HAS BROUGHT ME LIFE
I KNOW THAT IT IS FINISHED

I WILL NOT BOAST IN ANYTHING
NO GIFTS NO POWER NO WISDOM
BUT I WILL BOAST IN JESUS CHRIST
HIS DEATH AND RESURRECTION
WHY SHOULD I GAIN FROM HIS REWARD
I CANNOT GIVE AN ANSWER
BUT THIS I KNOW WITH ALL MY HEART
HIS WOUNDS HAVE PAID MY RANSOM

THE FATHER'S SONG

I HAVE HEARD SO MANY SONGS
LISTENED TO A THOUSAND TONGUES
BUT THERE IS ONE THAT SOUNDS
ABOVE THEM ALL

THE FATHER'S SONG THE FATHER'S LOVE
YOU SUNG IT OVER ME
AND FOR ETERNITY IT'S WRITTEN ON MY HEART

HEAVEN'S PERFECT MELODY
THE CREATOR'S SYMPHONY
YOU ARE SINGING OVER ME THE FATHER'S SONG

HEAVEN'S PERFECT MYSTERY
THE KING OF LOVE HAS SENT FOR ME
AND NOW YOU'RE SINGING OVER ME THE
FATHER'S SONG

THE FATHER'S SONG THE FATHER'S LOVE
YOU SUNG IT OVER ME
AND FOR ETERNITY IT'S WRITTEN ON MY HEART

END NOTES

Chapter 1.

1. Robert H Stein. *Baker's Evangelical Dictionary of Biblical Theology.* Ed. Walter A. Elwell. (Grand Rapids, Baker Books, 1996) (Bible study tools.com)

2. Carroll W.H. *History of Christendom, Vol. 2* (Christendom Press, 2004) *p.10.*
   (See also; James Strong Cyclopedia of Biblical, Theological and Ecclesiastical Literature. 7 p.45)

3. R. Dawkins. *The God Delusion.* (UK Bantam Books, 2006) *p.51.*

Chapter 2.

4. Terence Rattigan. *(1946 English play based on an incident from the Edwardian Era. From the movie, 'The Winslow Boy.'* (Sony Classic Pictures, 1999)

Chapter 4.

5. Christopher D. Hudson. *100 Names of God Daily Devotional.* (Rose Publishing, 2015 CA) *(See also Strong's Concordance)*

6. Thomas R Schreiner. *The King In His Beauty.* (Grand Rapids, Baker Academic. Baker Publishing Group, 2013) *prologue. p.14.*

Chapter 7.

7. 'Shanah.' *NAS Exhaustive Concordance.* *Strong's Concordance.*

8. Dr. Ernest F. Crocker. *When Oceans Roar.* (Australia, Authentic Media Ltd, 2016) *pp. 153-154.*

Chapter 8.

9. Jen Wilkin. *In His Image.* (Wheaton, Crossway, 2018) *pp. 73-74.*

10. Luther's Works and Large Catechism.
(Abbr. from Michael Reeves. *The Good God.* (MK, Paternoster; Authentic Media Ltd, 2012) *pp. 59-60.*

Chapter 10.

11. C. S. Lewis. *Mere Christianity, rev.ed.* (New York: Macmillan Publishing Company, first paperback edition, 1960) *p.146.*

Chapter 12.

12. Benny Hinn. *The Biblical Road to Blessing.* (USA, Thomas Nelson Publishers, Nashville, 1997) *pp. 18-19.*

Conclusion.

13. Philip Yancey. *Vanishing Grace.* (London, Hodder & Stoughton, 2014) *p.56.*

Reflection.

* Adm. by Capitol CMG Publishing worldwide excl. UK & Europe, admin by Integrity Music, part of the David C Cook family, songs@integritymusic.com

COVENANT - OBSERVATIONS OF A SOUND MIND

Since the writing of this book, I have felt challenged to expand further the concept of 'Covenant' as explored briefly in this book.

There is a deep and meaningful purpose in the Covenants as laid out in the Bible, which are still understood far more fully by nations such as in the Middle East and in Africa than in our western culture today.

These are important matters that really do matter to us when we come to a living faith in God, and they need to be absorbed into our thinking and our way of living, both in natural and spiritual terms.

So I have commenced this journey of the amazing truths of Covenant as expressed by the Hebrew people of the Bible and displayed wonderfully by the gift of the blessing of grace by The Heavenly Father.

I know that this is likely to throw up a variety of controversial thoughts and attitudes as we go along, but what is life without different opinions and perspectives?

If you have enjoyed this book, look out for following one, the study of Covenant. Phil

Lightning Source UK Ltd.
Milton Keynes UK
UKHW010624040821
388229UK00002B/46